Crime and Punishment

Pensées

The Great Divorce

Christian Perfection

A Taste of the Classics

SUMMARIZED BY KENNETH D. BOA

Biblica Publishing
We welcome your questions and comments.

USA 1820 Jet Stream Drive, Colorado Springs, CO 80921
www.authenticbooks.com
India Logos Bhavan, Medchal Road, Jeedimetla Village, Secunderabad
500 055, A.P.

A Taste of the Classics, Volume Three
ISBN-13: 978-1-93406-812-0

12 11 10 / 6 5 4 3 2 1

Published in 2010 by Biblica

A catalog record for this book is available through the Library of Congress.

Printed in the United States of America

Contents

Preface

Christians have a rich heritage of devout saints and brilliant thinkers, many of whom have left us their writings. Those with access to these writings have a treasure trove to help them along their journey of faith.

However, many of us lead frenetic lives that don't leave time for reflection, let alone engagement with some of the best Christian literature from across the generations. Dr. Kenneth Boa has helpfully summarized a number of these classics to give you a taste of what you may be missing. You may find deep refreshment in this book. Or, as with any sampler platter, you may discover a morsel you would delight to savor again. Perhaps you could then pick up the original work with a framework already in place to help you immediately engage the classic. Regardless of how you use this book, we hope your faith will be enriched through the considerable insights of generations before us.

A note on method: Dr. Boa cites numerous passages from each book. Because he proceeds through a book from beginning to end, we have chosen not to cite page numbers. This will create a more pleasant reading experience for you, and you will be able to locate passages from each book by the cues the author gives here.

Since the primary audience for this book is American, we have changed spellings to what is commonly accepted in the United States. However, we have left the original style and capitalization for each author. There are some points where authors used dubious capitalization, but we have chosen not to note them (using [sic]), again for ease of reading. Poetry is usually set in prose, for the sake of space. In this case, the initial capital letter in a line of poetry has been lowercased. The following editions are cited in this book:

Dostoevsky, Feodor. *Crime and Punishment*. Ed. George Gibian. New York: W. W. Norton & Company, 1989.

Pascal, Blaise. *The Mind on Fire* [*Pensées*]. Ed. James M. Houston. Portland: Multnomah Press, 1989.
Also, *Christianity for Modern Pagans: Pascal's Pensées.* Ed. Peter Kreeft. San Francisco: Ignatius Press, 1993.

Lewis, C. S. *The Great Divorce*. New York: HarperCollins, 2001.

Fénelon, François. *Christian Perfection*. Minneapolis: Bethany House Publishers, 1975.

Special thanks are due to Cindy Barnwell, who helped Dr. Boa edit and enrich the manuscript for publication.

FYODOR DOSTOYEVSKY

Crime and Punishment

Introduction

Among the most significant of all modern novels is Dostoyevsky's *Crime and Punishment*. Its author, Fyodor Mikhaylovich Dostoyevsky, was born on October 30, 1821. He was the son of a surgeon, the second of seven children, and grew up in Moscow. As a young man, he became involved with a socialist group called the Petrashevsky Circle. He and several other group members were eventually arrested, imprisoned by the government, and accused of seditious activities. On December 22, 1849, they were lined up before a firing squad, but at the last moment, the czar commuted their death sentences to a sentence of seven years hard labor in a Siberian prison camp. During those years young Dostoyevsky suffered from worsening fits of epilepsy. While ill, he spent many hours reading a copy of the New Testament, hoping to find some comfort or encouragement. Those prison years profoundly shaped his life, for when he finally returned to Moscow in 1859 and began to write again, his themes dealt with the struggles between traditional Christianity (in particular, Russian Orthodoxy) and the increasing secularism and rationalism of the Western world.

Dostoyevsky endured a period of tremendous personal turmoil both during and after his release from prison, whereby his family became virtually destitute. Throughout his adult life, he struggled with debt and an addiction to gambling. Following the death of his first wife, he married a younger woman, and they went off to Europe from 1867 to 1871, partly to escape the hounding of creditors. His second wife enabled him to pull away from those vices and to get back on a sound financial footing. The publication of *Crime and Punishment* in 1866 also contributed to their financial stability. From 1866 to 1880 was the period of the creation of his greatest works: *Crime and Punishment* appeared in 1866; *The Idiot* in 1868; *The Possessed* in 1872; and finally his masterpiece, *The Brothers Karamazov*, in 1880. Each of these books, in varying ways, portrays the struggle between an atheistic, utopian ideology on the one hand and a Christian worldview on the other. Exploring these themes and their implications became a pattern in his work.

Dostoyevsky knew well that ideas always have consequences, something he labored to convey in *Crime and Punishment*. Much thought preceded the writing of this novel. He created three large notebooks full of material before finally sitting down to actually write; these have, in fact, been published as accompanying notes to the book. Initially, as was often the case in the nineteenth century, this novel was serialized, which means it was published in monthly installments as it was being written.

Over the years Dostoyevsky has become renowned not only as a novelist but also as a literary psychologist of sorts. In his understanding of human nature and the strata of the subconscious, he was clearly ahead of his time. Indeed, he was prescient in his anticipation of future worldviews in terms of what later transpired in the Soviet political sphere, and he foresaw the potentially catastrophic effects of totalitarianism, particularly its reduced value for human life and freedom.

The fact that Dostoyevsky's worldview is decidedly Christian cannot be overlooked. Faith and religion do not occupy a merely peripheral role in his novels; rather, faith is central to understanding Dostoyevsky's themes and purposes. He seems to have anticipated Freud's idea of the subconscious, even the emerging themes of *Eros* (the life drive/instinct) and *Thanatos* (the death drive/instinct), terminology that Freud later employed to describe what he believed were two elemental and oppositional forces of existence. Dostoyevsky was well aware of such conflicting types of forces, as is evident in his presentation of the novel's protagonist. His novel was also significant to many who subscribed to the existentialist movement of the twentieth century because he depicts the human condition as a confrontation with mortality, despair, and the anxiety of choice.

Plot Overview

The setting of the novel is nineteenth-century St.

Petersburg, Russia, and the plot chronicles the premeditated murders of an old, miserly pawnbroker and her younger half sister by a destitute student named Rodion Romanovitch Raskolnikov. Dostoyevsky brilliantly portrays and develops the emotional, physical, and mental states that precede, accompany, and follow these heinous murders. In essence, this novel paints a portrait of the nature of guilt and explores the foundations of morality.

The novel's unique plot takes place predominantly in the mind of its conflicted protagonist. Raskolnikov's name is derived from the Russian root *raskol*, meaning "schism" or "split," and this is precisely the character's dilemma. A student and intellectual, Raskolnikov (or Rodya, as he is nicknamed) has embraced nihilistic philosophy and asserts that law is merely a human construct, and guilt nothing more than a self-induced state.

He hypothesizes that the reason so many criminal acts are unsuccessful is not because they are intrinsically wrong but because society has conditioned lawbreakers to feel guilt, and guilt produces "a failure of the will and reasoning power by a childish and phenomenal heedlessness, at the very instant when prudence and caution are most essential." He further argues that "this eclipse of reason and failure of willpower attacked a man like a disease, developed gradually and reached its highest point just before the perpetration of the crime, continued with equal violence at the moment of the crime . . . and then passed off like any other disease."

Yet Raskolnikov is perplexed on one major point of his theory: "whether the disease gives rise to the crime, or whether the crime [arises] from its own peculiar nature." It is via this postulate that Dostoyevsky begins his exploration of moral law through the character of Raskolnikov and his divided mind.

As Raskolnikov is introduced in chapter 1, his internal conflict becomes immediately evident. Dostoyevsky describes him as "acutely aware of his fears." As he engages in conversations within his own mind, the reader gradually learns of the character's radical theory: "I want to attempt a thing *like that* and am frightened by these trifles. . . . Hmm . . . yes, all is in a man's hands and he lets it all slip from cowardice, that's an axiom. . . . Am I capable of *that*? Is *that* serious?" (italics mine).

Despite its initial ambiguity, his plan soon becomes apparent; he desires to prove his theory that all morality is relative and that some people are superior to others. He has even devised a potential test of it—a perfect murder. He rationalizes that such a murder would permit him to see if he is one of those exceptional individuals who possess the intellect—and therefore the right—to defy law rather than submit to it. His prospective victim is a cruel, old woman, Alyona the pawnbroker, who inflicts harm and misery on others and seems to produce nothing of value herself.

As Rodya wanders the St. Petersburg streets debating his idea, he stops at a tavern. There he meets a pathetic, drunken civil servant by the name of Marmeladov, who attaches himself to Rodya. Unsolicited, Marmeladov gives his new acquaintance a brief history of his wretched life, explaining that his alcoholism and gambling have destroyed his career, his marriage, and his family. Marmeladov even admits that he has allowed his only daughter, a sixteen-year-old girl named Sonya, to prostitute herself in order to provide food for the family, yet even this dire situation has not motivated him to stop drinking, for he is drinking with money Sonya earned through prostitution.

Ironically, Marmeladov asserts that Sonya is a sweet child who does not want to defile herself in this way, but her love for her father, stepmother, and stepsiblings surpasses her concern for herself, just as Marmeladov's self-interest surpasses his concern for everything else. Although repulsed by the man, Raskolnikov becomes something of a family benefactor, motivated by pity to give them money occasionally.

A few days later, Raskolnikov carries out the test of his theory; however, his act is characterized by blunders and oversights rather than perfection. Despite the flaws in his plan and the mistakes he makes, including killing an unintended second victim, Raskolnikov manages to get away with his crime. Yet following the murders, he goes into seclusion and becomes ill for four days, growing increasingly paranoid that he is suspected of the crime and imagining that everyone already knows about his connection to it. This fear and guilt lead to a kind of insanity and growing disconnection from reality, and his mental and physical state mirrors the very affects of crime he had previously noted.

It is only after Raskolnikov confesses to the murders later in the novel that is it possible for him to be expiated. He is then sent to Siberia to do hard labor and while there discovers that life *can* have hope, purpose, and meaning.

Several vital subplots also run through the novel. Dostoyevsky presents the tragedy of the Marmeladov family, the dire economic plight of Raskolnikov's widowed mother and unmarried sister, the unrelenting pursuit of Raskolnikov by a police detective, the manipulations of the dysfunctional Svidrigailov, and the unwavering friendship extended to Raskolnikov by his friend, Razumihkin. Each of these subplots serves an important philosophical and literary function in the novel.

The novel concludes first with Raskolnikov's confession of his crimes and subsequent imprisonment and then with his abrupt repentance at the very end of the epilogue. Only in the final two pages of the novel does he finally yield to grace, personified by Sonya, and receive new life and hope. This is an important point, and we will return to it later in our discussion.

Characterization

Dostoyevsky employs a complex array of characters, foremost of whom is Raskolnikov, the novel's troubled protagonist. Raskolnikov rationalizes his actions in terms of his theory as he tries to ignore his own conscience, moral law, and relationships. Throughout much of the novel, he tries to forge an identity for himself, to validate his existence by creating, in a way, a kind of secular *kairos*. *Kairos* is a Greek word that translates as an opportune moment—some decisive event. Raskolnikov seeks such a defining moment to authenticate his exceptionality and superiority. He hypothesizes that the murder of the pawnbroker will be that defining event and an affirmation that he exists above social mores and moral law.

Yet even as Rodya speculates, his conscience is conflicted. He argues back and forth with himself about the validity of his theory. He abandons his plan and then returns to it. He argues that morality is subjective and then asserts that providence led him to the murder. All of this indicates the fundamental fallacy of his worldview. Despite his protestations against an absolute, universal moral law, in his heart he knows and believes in law.

At one point prior to the murders, he sits drinking in a tavern and overhears a conversation between two men. They are discussing the very theory he espouses. The one man puts forth a hypothetical situation that precisely mirrors Rodya's plan. He suggests it might be permissible to kill a worthless individual, such as Alyona the pawnbroker, for the benefit of the majority: "Kill her, take her money and with the help of it devote oneself to the service of humanity and the good of all. What do you think, would not one tiny crime be wiped out by thousands of good deeds? For one life thousands would be saved from corruption and decay. . . . —it's simple arithmetic!"

Raskolnikov is "violently agitated" when he overhears these men and wonders why he happened to be in that tavern at just the time the men were discussing his theory. The narrator goes on to say, "This trivial talk in a tavern had an immense influence on him in his later action; as though there had really been in it something preordained, some guiding hint."

Now this statement has great significance. Rodya's exceptional-man theory is predicated on the assumption that there are no absolutes—that man is alone in the universe and therefore creates his own morality. Yet in ironic inconsistency, he supposes preordination or some sort of guiding force is leading him to the murder. This stands in direct opposition to the theory. Either man makes his own moral path because there is nothing permanent or eternal to guide him, or man exists within a moral framework that he neither created nor controls. Rodya would break from moral law while depending on the security of a preordained path. He struggles with this sort of inconsistency throughout the entire novel, before and after his crime.

Dostoyevsky next introduces the complex character of Sonya Marmeladov as a primary refutation of Rodya's reductionistic view of man. Sonya, as we mentioned earlier, is the daughter of an alcoholic, unemployed civil servant. Her mother is dead, and her father is remarried to a widow, Katerina Ivanovna, who regards him as degraded and worthless. The reader learns that Marmeladov's wife married him only because she had three young children to support and nowhere else to turn.

Marmeladov has gambled and drunk away the family's resources, and at Katerina's request, sixteen-year-old Sonya has begun prostituting herself to support her father and stepfamily. The reader's sympathies are aroused by Marmeladov's own description of his daughter's dire circumstances.

As he sits drinking with money procured by her ruin, he describes Sonya's response to her stepmother's request: "Katerina Ivanovna, am I really to do a thing like that?" Ironically, at the very time of the conversation, Marmeladov, Sonya's father, is lying drunk on a cot in the corner of the room. He overhears his wife's demand, yet he does not intervene. He even watches as his daughter returns three hours later, and relates that "[she] did not utter a word, she did not even look at [Katerina], she simply picked up our big green . . . shawl, put it over her head and face and lay down on the bed with her face to the wall; and her little shoulders and her body kept shuddering." Marmeladov then admits to his listeners in the tavern that "here I, her own father, here I took thirty kopecks of that money for a drink! And I am drinking it! And I have already drunk it!"

Throughout the narrative, Sonya demonstrates a Christlike submission of her will. She gives herself on behalf of those who do not merit or even appreciate her sacrifice. In describing her selflessness, her stepmother declares, "What a heart she has, what a girl she is! . . . She'd sell her last rag, she'd go barefoot to help you if you needed it, that's what she is! She has the yellow passport because my children were starving, she sold herself for us!" In her, the reader sees a "type" of Christ, who, as Scripture says, came not to be served, but to serve and give his life for others.

This said, it is vitally important that the reader evaluate Sonya's moral condition according to the terms set by the author. Nowhere in the novel does Dostoyevsky excuse Sonya's immorality on the basis of either her desperation or her pure motives. To do so would be unbiblical and thematically inconsistent. Notice that she is not forced into prostitution by Katerina; she *yields* to Katerina's urging—an important distinction. Like Christ, she gives herself of her own free will; she chooses to sacrifice herself, understanding the consequences of that choice. Yes, she is motivated by love, but even she never relies on that love motivation to excuse her behavior. In fact, later in the novel, she makes it plain that she depends solely on Providence to judge her soul. She does not attempt to usurp God's power with her will; rather, she submits her will to both man and God and trusts God for the outcome.

With the introduction of the three characters—Rodya,

Marmeladov, and Sonya—Dostoyevsky personifies man's three-part nature of intellect, instinct, and soul. Rodya, who is listening to Marmeladov's ramblings, is determined to live only according to reason and will. Marmeladov has given in to his basest animal instincts and is living as a beast, incapable of love or altruism. Sonya, however, has submitted both reason and instinct to love and chosen to look beyond herself to the needs of others. Her name fits her role, for it is derived from the Greek word *sophia*, meaning "wisdom."

It is in the context of this triangulation that the plot occurs. Rodya determines to test his theory that morality is merely a man-made construct. He works out his plan to kill the old and vile pawnbroker, Alyona, who, in his and the public's estimation, produces nothing but misery. Dostoyevsky uses the character of Rodya to depict the moral tension and deterioration that occur when man attempts to misuse his will and reason to obtain power. He also adds another very significant character to the plot.

Svidrigailov, a wealthy, middle-aged resident of St. Petersburg, provides another perspective on the will-to-power theory. In fact, he serves as a foil of sorts for both Raskolnikov and Marmeladov. While Raskolnikov aspires to act only in accordance with his own will, he frequently wavers. For instance, he impulsively gives money to the Marmeladov family and then regrets the irrationality of those impulses. He cradles the bloody and dying Marmeladov and provides for his funeral; then after the fact, he wonders what prompted him to do this. In contrast, Svidrigailov entertains no such impulses. He consistently seeks his own gratification without consideration of anyone else.

Furthermore, just as Marmeladov, the other sensate character of the novel, is enslaved to alcohol, Svidrigailov is enslaved to lust. But unlike Marmeladov, who claims he only drinks to increase his own suffering—a misguided and futile attempt at penance—Svidrigailov exhibits no remorse. He is an unabashed adulterer and pedophile who preys on young women, is believed to have murdered his own wife, and attempts to bribe Rodya's sister, Dunya, in exchange for a sexual encounter. In contrast to Rodya's inconsistent attempts to live solely by reason, Svidrigailov applies his will to a determined attempt to live solely by sensation. In that sense, he is the only consistent nihilist of the novel—the only person who truly lives out the will-to-power theory to the end.

Several other significant characters also serve to convey Dostoyevsky's complex themes. Rodya's friend, Razumihkin, represents an appropriate balance of man's three dimensions. He employs reason purposefully, subjugates his will to a moral standard, and as a result is able to interact with humanity freely.

One of the most significant characters of the novel is Porfiry Petrovich, a police detective who functions as a symbol of the law and whose role complements Sonya's. Although Porfiry lacks the hard evidence to substantiate an arrest or conviction, he gathers enough circumstantial evidence to conclude that Rodya is the murderer of the two victims, Alyona and Lizaveta. He is particularly fascinated by a paper Rodya had written concerning morality—not because he agrees with Rodya's thesis but because he hopes to intervene and correct his reasoning errors. He baits Rodya by reminding him of his assertion in his paper that "there are certain persons who . . . have a perfect right to commit breaches of morality and crimes, and that the law is not for them." He goes on to note that according to Rodya's article, "All men are divided into 'ordinary' and 'extraordinary'. Ordinary men have to live in submission, have no right to transgress the law, because, don't you see, they are ordinary. But extraordinary men have a right to commit . . . breaches of morals . . . not an official right, but an inner right to decide in his own conscience to overstep . . . certain obstacles."

Porfiry clearly recognizes the danger of Rodya's philosophical path and seeks to guide him back via the law. Throughout the novel his character functions as a parallel to Sonya's; she represents grace via Christ, and he represents the law as the tutor to lead man to Christ (Galatians 3). This is affirmed in the very limitations of Porfiry's role. While he knows of Rodya's guilt and causes him to feel it acutely, he can do little more than convict Rodya's conscience of his moral breach; he cannot bring Rodya to repentance, a point we will discuss shortly when we explore the novel's themes.

Katerina, the wife of Marmeladov and stepmother of Sonya, also plays a significant role, serving in a tragic capacity. While Sonya's suffering stems from her selfless love of others, Katerina's suffering stems from self-aggrandizement. She regards herself as the hapless victim of two unfortunate marriages, takes out her anger and frustration on her family, and ultimately trusts in the redemptive value of her own suffering rather than in Christ. On her deathbed she refuses last rites by a priest, misguidedly asserting, "I have no sins." Like Rodya, she places her faith in herself. In an antithetical function, she contrasts Sonya's utter dependence on Providence.

She also provides the reader with a poignant example of the doom Rodya faces apart from grace.

There are many other characters in this novel, but these seven best convey Dostoyevsky's thematic purposes. It is through them and their intersecting lives that the author establishes his refutation of rationalism, totalitarianism, and nihilism. It is through Sonya that he builds the case for Christianity as the only plausible and functional worldview. And it is in the epilogue that he solidifies the contrast between the futility of the will-to-power theory with God's offer of redemptive grace, which allows man's will to function effectively.

Critical Interpretation

Despite the clarity with which Dostoyevsky presents his themes, his novel has frequently been misunderstood, especially by those who fail to examine it within the framework of its author's Christian worldview. People have struggled over how to approach the novel, recognizing the greatness of it, but disagreeing over how to interpret it.

One early critic described the work in terms of the phenomena of contemporary social life and basically reduced it to a treatise on economic theory—poverty and so forth—and deliberately chose to ignore Dostoyevsky's beliefs and the stature of the work as an aesthetic achievement. This reminds me of what many people do today, where the issue becomes the mindset of the critic and not the intent of the author. Such deconstructionism is hardly new. And while as this particular critic noted, the novel addresses the economic implications of radical individualism and utilitarianism, its themes rise beyond mere economic significance. Yes, Dostoyevsky attacks, for instance, social utopian economic theory through the character of Pyotr Petrovich Luzhin, the fiancé of Rodya's sister, but this is not a central theme of the novel. Despite his inclusion of such economic discussions, Dostoyevsky's central theme deals with an issue of far greater significance: the state of the soul.

Another critic, by the name of Strakhov, asserted that the novel was a case study of the conflict between life and theory. Again, it is true that Rodya's personal schism reflects such a conflict, but his life and struggle depict far more. Rodya does not merely fail to reconcile a theory with its practical application; his theory fails because it is intrinsically flawed—Dostoyevsky's central point.

Yet another critic, writing in the 1890s, spoke about the book as a psychological portrait of Raskolnikov; he was one of the first to analyze the dream sequences that play such a significant role in the development of the novel's themes. Yet even this analysis falls short, for while the novel *is* psychological, it is much more. Again, it is an examination of the plight of the soul, not merely the mind.

A number of critics have drawn comparisons between the narrative and classical tragedy, arguing that Dostoyevsky essentially intended to write a tragedy that depicted a Promethean sort of man attempting to stand against fate and divinity. Such critics note that the novel is divided into an introductory section (or prologue), five primary sections (or acts), and an epilogue; and they then attempt to fit the novel into a sort of dramatic pattern.

While this interpretive approach comes much closer to

the truth than many others, there are a number of problems with such an analysis. Although the primary plot focuses on the pride-induced downfall of Raskolnikov, the novel makes several clear breaks from the tragic formula. First, the law is incapable of holding Rodya accountable for his crime; he escapes its clutches yet later *chooses* to confess his crime when he can no longer stand his state of isolation and alienation. Second, the epilogue defies the tragic pattern, making the novel a comedy, in the strict sense of the term, rather than a tragedy. The classic pattern involves a person of significance who, as a result of a willful moral breach, suffers destruction. In contrast, Raskolnikov is redeemed, not destroyed. The novel ends with the promise of new life, not despair or death.

Themes

The central theme of alienation versus fellowship runs throughout Dostoyevsky's novel and serves to convey the truth of its gospel message. While defiance to law isolates and alienates, the promise and hope of the gospel are restoration of right relationship—fellowship—with both God and man. From the moment of his crime until his public confession of it, Raskolnikov experiences an oppressive sense of alienation. This is why he feels such an overwhelming urge to confess his crime long before he actually does so. To confess would be to rejoin with society through submission to moral law. Far more significant than Dostoyevsky's deconstruction of the will-to-power theory, however, is his presentation of the gospel—his juxtaposition of a false worldview with truth.

Here the work's title proves helpful, for it sums up man's

dilemma. While many people, the novel's protagonist included, would like to believe that crime and punishment are no more than civil/societal constructs that maintain order in society, the author reveals the narrowness of that view through the lives of his characters. None of them adhere to the constructs of society. Marmeladov drinks, gambles, shirks his duties and family, and tolerates the ruin of his daughter. Alyona exploits the most desperate members of society, hoards wealth without enjoyment of it, and savagely abuses her weak half sister. Katerina inflicts harm on her children, husband, and stepdaughter in a selfish attempt to exercise control. Svidrigailov sexually exploits young girls, leverages power and wealth for personal gratification, and kills his own wife. Rodya plots and executes two murders. Sonya illegally prostitutes herself to provide an income for her family. Dostoyevsky's characterization demonstrates Romans 3:10: "There is none righteous, not even one." This is not merely a novel about the consequences of breaking laws; it is a novel about the consequences of breaking *the* law.

Therefore, Dostoyevsky's apparently sudden redemption of his protagonist in the epilogue has troubled many a reader who failed to understand the centrality of the novel's gospel theme, prominent literary critic Harold Bloom among them. Bloom has argued that the epilogue undermines the nearly flawless brilliance of the novel, and he has accused its author of "tendentiousness," asserting that "Dostoyevsky is superb at beginnings, astonishing at middle developments, but oddly weak at endings" (*How to Read and Why*, "Crime and Punishment"). He arrives at this faulty conclusion because he, like many others, fails to grasp Dostoyevsky's thematic purpose. Not only is the epilogue essential to the narrative as a whole, but it provides the author's final response to rationalism, social utopianism, utilitarianism, and the nihilistic void: the gospel of Christ.

While, as Bloom notes, Rodya's titanic struggle of the will mirrors that of the tragic hero, particularly Macbeth, Shakespeare's character ultimately defies order and dooms himself via his immoral elevation of his will. Rodya does no such thing, although for a time he follows a similar path. Like Macbeth, Rodya pursues the gratification of his will against his better judgment. This is seen perhaps most clearly through his recollection of the mare dream prior to the murders; it is, in a sense, Dostoyevsky's version of the bloody dagger vision of *Macbeth*.

In his dream Rodya is a very young child walking home with his father when they encounter a group of drunken peasants, one of whom is driving a small cart pulled by an old, sickly mare. In his irrational state, the driver offers to give the others a ride, yet it is apparent that this is beyond the capacity of the mare. When she proves unable to move the cart, the driver begins to beat her, working himself into a frenzied rage. He ultimately kills the mare with an axe, asserting his right to do so as her owner.

Rodya's child-self recognizes the injustice of this act and is horrified by the brutality of the drunken man. He wakes from the dream breathless and terrified and then exclaims, "Good God! . . . Can it be, can it be, that I shall really take an axe, that I shall strike her [his prospective murder victim] on the head, split her skull open . . . that I shall tread in the sticky warm blood, break the lock, steal and tremble; hide, all spattered in the blood . . . with the axe. . . . Good God, can it be?" At this moment in the novel, Rodya, like Macbeth prior to his fateful crime, understands the horror of what he is about to do. And like Macbeth, he misuses reason to justify the gratification of his will. Both men provide the reader with unprecedented glimpses into the mind about to willfully doom itself. Rodya is neither blind to the brutality of his proposed crime nor ignorant of its potential consequences, yet he perseveres in his futile course of action.

Prior to the crime, Raskolnikov labors to rationalize his actions: "He had thought about the main point, but he had set the details aside until he had convinced himself." In other words, he actually works to convince himself to follow through with the test of his theory. Dostoyevsky then goes on to say,

> And yet it would seem that his analysis, in the sense of a moral solution to the question, was concluded; his casuistry had the cutting edge of a razor, and he could no longer find any conscious objections [to the murder] in his own mind. But in the last resort he simply did not believe himself and obstinately, slavishly groped for objections on all sides, as if he were driven by some compulsion. His reactions during this last day, which had come upon him so unexpectedly and settled everything at one stroke, were almost completely mechanical, as though someone had taken his hand and pulled him along irresistibly, blindly, with supernatural strength and without objection. It was as if a part of his clothing had been caught in the wheel of a machine and he

was being dragged into it.

What an apt and vivid description, is it not? Even as Rodya is trying to rationalize his crime by somehow asserting himself as greater than the rest of men, his mind and conscience are engaged in agonizing conflict. He recognizes that free will permits man to exercise power, but the mare dream also reminds him that such abuses of power are hideous.

Prior to his crime Rodya repeatedly senses that he is fated or preordained to carry out this experiment, yet this flies in the very face of his theory. How can such a thing as fate or providence exist if moral constructs have no basis in divinity? If man exists in an unguided universe, subject only to his own will and his own capacity to gratify that will, there is no fate—no preordinance or providence to guide him either to or away from crime. Yet Rodya repeatedly acknowledges such a force, saying at one point that he senses "there had really been in it something preordained, some guiding hint."

Dostoyevsky then drives home the foolishness of Rodya's crime, both at the actual crime scene and in the consequences that ensue. He carefully illustrates the crime's degenerative effect on the will. From the moment Rodya determines to carry out his "experiment," he spirals into irrationality. In other words, he loses the capacity to employ his will purposefully. Chapter 7 of part I is peppered with phrases that illustrate this: "[a] giddiness came over him"; "He was in a sort of delirium"; "he was filled with despair"; "[he] was only dimly conscious of himself now"; "He was not fully conscious." The chapter concludes with this telling statement: "Scraps and shreds of thoughts were simply swarming in his brain, but he could not catch at one, he could not rest on one, in spite of all his efforts."

Then part II begins with his admission that "he thought he was going mad." From the moment Rodya determines to do his own will until he finally submits his will in the epilogue, he experiences torment and despair. Like Macbeth, he experiences "scorpions of the mind" and begins to comprehend that it would be better to destroy himself than to "dwell in doubtful joy" (*Macbeth* III. ii). But unlike Macbeth, he eventually embraces grace, escaping the ruin of the classical tragic pattern.

In communicating his central themes, Dostoyevsky repeatedly links drunkenness with his presentation of the will-to-power theory. Man's boundless ambition to elevate the will to supremacy is likened to the effects of drunkenness. The literal intoxication of Marmeladov, the sexual intoxication of Svidrigailov, and the moral intoxication of Raskolnikov impede their ability to reason and act effectively. From the moment he commits his crime until he finally repents of it, Raskolnikov's reason is inebriated. In fact, in part II, chapter 1, he admits as much, saying, "If anyone had come in, what would he have thought? That I'm drunk." A few moments later he laments, "My reason's deserting me—simply!" Dostoyevsky describes the state of his newly created criminal: "The conviction that all his faculties, even memory, and the simplest power of reflection were failing him, began to be an insufferable torture." From this time on, Rodya is characterized by inner turmoil and overwhelmed by an impulse to confess his crime.

Dostoyevsky once stated that if there is no God, then all things are permissible. This novel, more than any of his other works, serves to illustrate the truth of that statement. While Rodya strives to live above all law, the characters of Porfiry and Sonya function to reassert the immutability of the law. Throughout the novel, the guilt-ridden Raskolnikov is pursued by both law and grace, law in the person of Porfiry and grace through the person of Sonya. While he manages to resist both for a time, it is ultimately alienation that induces him to confess his crime. Yet it is critical that the reader notices that Rodya confesses first to Sonya, the Christ figure of the novel, and *then* to Porfiry.

Here Dostoyevsky brilliantly depicts the arguments of Galatians 3, where Paul states, "If a law had been given which was able to impart life, then righteousness would indeed have been based on law. . . . The Law has become our tutor to lead us to Christ" (vv. 21, 24). While the law convicts Rodya of his guilt, it is insufficient to bring him to repentance. Porfiry represents the law and is the person who attempts to use reason to bring Raskolnikov to the realization of his own crime and an admission of it. Porfiry recognizes that he is dealing with a guilty man and has a very clear plan to bring Raskolnikov to the point of admission of guilt.

Porfiry says,

> Now, if I leave one gentlemen quite alone, if I don't arrest him or worry him in any way, but if he knows, or at least suspects, every minute of every hour, that I know everything down to the last detail, and am watching him day and night with ceaseless vigilance, if he is always conscious of the weight of suspicion and fear, he is absolutely certain to lose his head. He will

> come to me of his own accord, and perhaps commit some blunder, which will provide, so to speak, mathematical proof, like two and two make four—and that is very satisfactory.

He goes on to say,

> What is running away? It's merely formal; the point is that he won't run away because he has no where to run to, but that psychologically he won't escape. What an expression. By a law of his nature he wouldn't escape, even if he had somewhere to escape to. Have you ever seen a moth with a candle? Well, he'll be just like that, he'll circle round me as if I were a candle: Freedom will no longer be a boon to him; he will begin to brood, he will get himself into a muddle, entangle his own feet in a net, and worry himself to death!

You could very well say, in an analogy to Galatians 3, that Porfiry represents the law as Paul describes the law: as a tutor that leads us to grace and to faith. He pokes and he prods at Raskolnikov; he questions and manipulates him until he finally understands and acknowledges his guilt.

What is significant, though, is that Rodya's confession is first made not to Porfiry, but to Sonya. This is significant because it shows the limitation of the law. It can only bring us to the point of conviction; it can reveal and convict one of sin, but it has no redemptive power. That is why Dostoyevsky has Raskolnikov make his confession first to the novel's Christ figure, who is given the priestly role of hearing that confession. While Porfiry can be credited with pricking his conscious, Sonya is the one who is involved in his actual redemption.

Yet even after he confesses to his crime and admits himself incapable of bearing the burden of alienation necessary to his extraordinary-man theory, Raskolnikov remains stubbornly convinced of the plausibility of his theory. Even in prison in Siberia "he did not repent of his crime." Instead "he raged at the grotesque blunders that had brought him to prison. . . . He thought over and criticized all his actions again and by no means found them so blundering and grotesque as they had seemed at the fatal time." He even asks himself, "In what way . . . was my theory stupider than others that have swarmed and clashed from the beginning of the world?"

Now as part of the response to this question, it is necessary to take a brief detour from the protagonist and examine the character of Svidrigailov, the consistent nihilist of the novel. While Rodya wavers in his adherence to his professed worldview, struggling between the moral tension of self-gratification and his need for fellowship, Svidrigailov pursues the will-to-power theory to its natural conclusion. A sexual addict, Svidrigailov determines to seduce Rodya's sister, Dunya; however, she refuses his advances and bribes, leaving his lust unsatiated. The will to power then offers only one option for the adherent who can no longer achieve gratification of the will: suicide. It is the ultimate assertion of the will in defiance to law and absolutes. In keeping with his worldview, Svidrigailov adheres to the will-to-power theory until he can no longer obtain what he wills; then he wills his own extinction.

This is something that Rodya is unwilling to do. Reflecting on Svidrigailov's suicide, he asks himself why he hadn't "killed himself? Why had he stood looking at the river and preferred to confess? Was the desire to live so strong and was it so hard to overcome it? Had not Svidrigailov overcome it, though he was afraid of death?" Yet something prevents Rodya from taking that final nihilistic leap, even though he has no conscious desire to live. Dostoyevsky uses this contrast between Rodya and Svidrigailov as part of his refutation of nihilism. In fact, in Svidrigailov, the consistent nihilist, its failure as a worldview is *most* evident. His life is reduced to a futile search for gratification as he gluts himself on sexual encounters without love, fulfillment, or satiation. His suicide reiterates the failure of his worldview, for it is not a triumph of the will but an indication of its inadequacy.

Thematic Significance of the Epilogue

The epilogue then continues with Dostoyevsky's refutation of nihilism. About one year into his eight-year sentence, Rodya becomes very ill for several weeks. While delirious from fever, he dreams that a terrible plague breaks out on every continent, producing devastating effects, effects that mirror those of rationalism and nihilism:

> Some new sorts of . . . microbes were endowed with intelligence and will. Men attacked by them became at once mad and furious. But never had men considered themselves so intellectual and so completely in possession of the truth as these sufferers, never had they considered their decisions, their scientific conclusions, their moral convictions so infallible.

> . . . Each thought that he alone had the truth and was wretched looking at the others. . . . They did not know how to judge and could not agree on what to consider evil and what good; they did not know whom to blame, whom to justify. Men killed each other in a sort of senseless spite. They gathered together in armies against one another, but even on the march the armies would begin attacking each other, the ranks would be broken and the soldiers would fall on each other. . . . The alarm bell was ringing all day long in the towns; men rushed together, but why they were summoned and who was summoning them no one knew. . . . Only a few men could be saved in the whole world. They were a pure, chosen people, destined to found a new race and a new life, to renew and purify the earth, but no one had seen these men, no one had heard their words and their voices.

This passage presents the novel's most overt attack on postmodern ideology. It foreshadows with uncanny accuracy some of the very horrors that utilitarianism, totalitarianism, and nihilism will later inflict in the twentieth century.

Significantly, it is after this dream that Raskolnikov finally repents. Symbolically, his repentance occurs after his fever has broken and his recovery has begun, just two weeks after Easter. This seems to suggest the author's answer to the question his character had posed way back at the outset of the novel: Does crime result from disease, or does crime produce some peculiar disease or ailment? From a Christian perspective, the answer is both. Human nature is predisposed to the sickness that is sin, but sin or crime itself sickens the soul similarly to how a virus attacks the body.

Just as obedience to law permits free interaction, or fellowship, so defiance of law produces isolation and alienation from society in a sort of mandatory sin quarantine. Although Raskolnikov claims to understand such alienation as the condition of the exceptional man's assertion of his will, he quickly learns he cannot long survive in such a state. In fact, it is his inability to cope with his alienation that provokes his confession.

Symbols and Motifs

The motif of sickness runs throughout the entire narrative. Raskolnikov is depicted as sickly and pale. He begins to feel ill even before he commits the murders, but afterward, he becomes feverish, delusional, and is bedridden for four days. Dostoyevsky uses the sickness motif to suggest a link between crime and illness, presenting crime (sin) as a sort of virus or disease.

Several of the novel's characters also struggle with illness. Katerina dies of consumption, Marmeladov's description suggests advanced liver failure and jaundice, and Rodya's mother, Pulcheria Alexandrovna, dies from a fever-related brain illness.

Finally, the plague dream related in the epilogue provides the clearest connection between the will-to-power concept and disease. Rodya dreams that a devastating plague causes men to feel intelligent and yet to actually lack rationality. The resulting confusion spreads across every continent, wreaking terrible consequences.

Another important motif in the novel has to do with fresh air and vegetation. Repeatedly, Raskolnikov complains of overwhelming feelings of suffocation and a desire for fresh air. St. Petersburg itself is depicted as stifling and dank. Rodya's cramped little room is particularly suffocating and stale. These images help to convey the oppressive and detrimental nature of the nihilistic worldview.

In the same vein as the stale air images are the space images. Ironically, while he is free, Rodya complains of feeling cramped, trapped, confined, and limited. Dostoyevsky repeatedly uses the metaphor of a square yard of space to articulate this feeling of confinement. While Rodya is physically free but overwhelmed by the guilt and alienation of his crime, he feels like he is confined within a square yard of space. Then ironically, when he is living in a tiny cell within a Siberian prison, he no longer feels that oppressive sense of confinement. With this contrast Dostoyevsky conveys another aspect of the nature of crime: it alienates and isolates. It metaphorically confines the criminal within the prison of his own conscience and guilt.

The recurring Lazarus allusion serves as the most important symbol of the entire novel, however, for Dostoyevsky uses it to communicate his central theme of the availability of new life in Christ. After his crime Rodya lies nearly unconscious for a period of four days. Likewise, Lazarus lay dead in his tomb for four days until being raised by Jesus. Rodya demands that Sonya read that passage in John 11 to him just a short time before he confesses to his crime. The fact that she reads the passage from a New Testament given her by Lizaveta is significant. Furthermore, Dostoyevsky does not merely allude to the biblical account of Lazarus's resuscitation; he includes the entire passage, word for word, thereby emphasizing its significance to his central theme.

While visiting Sonya, Raskolnikov sees an old, worn Russian translation of the New Testament in her room. "'Where is that about Lazarus,' he asks abruptly." She is very hesitant about this and does not want to read the account to him. He essentially demands it and says, "Read! I want you to. You used to read to Lizaveta." Now, Lizaveta, whom Rodya had murdered, had been Sonya's dear friend. In fact, they had exchanged crosses with one another, and Sonya later gives Lizaveta's cross to Raskolnikov. In obedience to Rodya's demand, "Sonya opened the book and found the place. Her hands shook, her voice failed. Twice she tried to begin, but could not utter the first word." Finally she begins to read the account.

She reaches the point where the Scripture says, "Jesus said unto her, 'I am the resurrection and the life: he that believeth in Me though he were dead, yet shall he live. And whosoever liveth and believeth in Me shall never die. Believest thou this?'" Sonya's voice trembles with emotion as she read of Christ's power over death. Yet Raskolnikov ironically fails to recognize himself in this passage. He, like Lazarus, is dead; he is blind; he is spiritually inert. He, like the Pharisees who witnessed Lazarus's restoration to life, still fails to grasp Christ's offer of redemption.

The text continues as Sonya reads with expectancy: "'And he, he who is also unbelieving, he also will hear in a moment. He also will believe'. 'Yes. Yes. Here and now', she dreamed and trembled with joyful expectancy. Jesus therefore again groaning in himself cometh to the grave. It was a cave and a stone lay upon it. Jesus said, 'Take ye away the stone'. Martha, the sister of him that was dead saith unto him, 'Lord, by this time he stinketh: for he has been dead four days'. Sonya strongly emphasized the word four." It was no accident that Raskolnikov lay nearly unconscious for precisely four days after the murder. Like the dead Lazarus, he is also stinking; he has been metaphorically dead since his crime and is need of resurrection.

Listen to how Dostoyevsky describes it: "Her feverish trembling continued. The candle-end had long since burned low in the twisted candlestick, dimly lighting the poverty-stricken room and the murderer and the harlot who had come together so strangely to read the eternal book." Again Dostoyevsky emphasizes the gospel message; the point is not the sin; the point is Christ. Whether the sin be harlotry or murder, Christ offers the solution.

Yet Raskolnikov is not yet ready to grasp that truth, for instead of repenting, he leaps up, saying that man must "break what must be broken, once for all, that's all, and take the suffering on oneself. . . . Freedom and power, and above all, power! Over all trembling creation and all the ant-heap! . . . That's the goal." Here he misses the point of Lazarus's restoration completely. Man is incapable of taking suffering on himself. Katerina and Marmeladov both tragically illustrate that. This is something only Sonya seems to grasp. It is not one's personal suffering that matters; it is that a sinless Christ suffered, died, and triumphed over sin that matters. The nihilistic goal is deification of self at the expense of rejection of the gospel hope—salvation through Christ's atonement for sin.

In keeping with his view of self-sufficiency, however, throughout the novel, Rodya supposes that he is some kind of a superman whose intellect frees him from the limitations that restrict the rest of humanity. He supposes he is a kind of Napoleon who, unlike ordinary men, can transcend moral boundaries. However, Dostoyevsky goes to great pains to refute his character's exceptional-man theory by portraying Raskolnikov's psychological schism before, during, and after the murders, as well as the physical and mental illness that attends his moral breach.

Raskolnikov's real punishment in this novel is not imprisonment; rather, it is his psychological torment. Dostoyevsky explores the psychology of the criminal and illustrates the disparity between Rodya's intellectual theory and inner turmoil. He experiences constant tension as he is pulled between his knowledge of right and wrong and the rationalistic, utilitarian theory that he uses to justify his actions.

In Rodya the author presents a character who seeks to affirm himself in a titanic self-assertion but who, ironically, is actually destroying himself. This becomes a theme that Dostoyevsky traces all the way through to the very end of the novel. In fact, he focuses more on the guilt than the crime itself, as well as on the fact that there are immutable moral laws that cannot be overcome merely by one's rationalization or determination.

Style

I am fascinated by the style of this novel. Dostoyevsky meticulously and repeatedly revised his works; I mentioned earlier his three notebooks in which he continually refined his understanding of his progress. Once he felt he knew what he wanted to write, he then dictated the novel, which is an achievement in itself.

It is also significant to note that he wrote a first draft of this text and later burned it because he did not like his choice of the first-person narrative. He didn't think it adequately communicated the complexity of the characters and plot. He then began the novel again and this time employed a third-person, limited-omniscient point of view. That allowed him to surround Raskolnikov with an aura of mystery; Raskolnikov himself is on the edge of sanity, and the reader is granted access to part of this internal dialogue that takes place.

In addition, Dostoyevsky brilliantly incorporates literary techniques such as suspense, coincidence, and foreshadowing. He also works creatively with time, suspending particular sequences so he can envelope a mystery in a small pocket of time. He uses the technique of the dramatic present to make passages vividly alive. He transforms his philosophical ideas into artistic material as he creates characters who are actually personifications of those ideas.

This is clearly a beautifully crafted novel, and I want to include just a sample of Dostoyevsky's craftsmanship. It is a description of a minor character, and it is an example of the eloquent prose that characterizes this novel. Dostoyevsky writes, "He was one of that countless and multifarious legion of nondescripts, putrescent abortions, and uninformed obstinate fools who instantly and infallibly attach themselves to the most fashionable current idea, with the immediate effect of vulgarizing it and of turning it into a ridiculous caricature any cause they serve, however sincerely." That is simply a brilliant bit of prose.

Conclusion

The cross serves as a recurrent symbol of redemptive suffering throughout Dostoyevsky's novel. From the beginning when Raskolnikov determines to seek his own salvation via the will, to Sonya's gift of Lizaveta's wooden cross, to Raskolnikov's confession at a crossroads and eventual recognition of the inadequacy of the will to save, the cross image is a unifying theme. It is fascinating to me that the gift of the cross impels and enables him to make his confession. Even his journey to confess functions as an allusion to the account of the crucifixion, for he falls to his knees in the town square before he turns himself in. There is a power in this, and it is significant that this is just an ordinary cross made of cypress wood. In other words, by accepting that cross he is admitting his dependency on it—that he is an ordinary man trapped under the weight and guilt of sin.

Yet as we reach the end of the novel where he is now in a Siberian prison, he still has not come to a state of repentance. He is still unwilling to admit the failure of his worldview: "How happy he would have been if he could have put the blame on himself! Then he could have borne anything, even shame and infamy. But although he judged himself severely, his lively conscience could find no particularly terrible guilt in his past, except a simple blunder." He rationalizes his ideology and seeks to justify his guilt. Continuing, he calls his crime and its consequences a blunder "that might have happened to anybody." Then Dostoyevsky says,

> He was ashamed precisely because he, Raskolnikov, had perished so blindly and hopelessly, with such dumb stupidity, by some decree of blind fate, and must humble himself and submit to the absurdity of that decree, if he wished to find any degree of peace. An objectless and undirected anxiety in the present and endless sacrifice, by which nothing would be gained, in the future, was all the world held for him. And what did it signify that in eight years he would be only thirty-two and still able to begin a new life? What would he have to live for? What could be his aim? What should he strive for; to live in order to exist? But he had been ready a thousand times before to sacrifice his existence for an idea.

That final phrase is incredibly important—"a hope, even for a fancy. Mere existence had always meant little to him; he had always desired more. Perhaps it was just because of the strength of his desires that he had considered himself a man to whom more was permitted than to others." Notice that he remains so committed to his stubborn will that he would willingly "sacrifice his existence for an idea."

Then, his repentance and resurrection into life occur as abruptly as Lazarus's literal restoration from death. John recounts how at Jesus' command, Lazarus returned to life and emerged from the tomb, even though he had been dead many days. Similarly, at the very end of the novel, Dostoyevsky paints a portrait of Rodya's similar redemption. Sonya comes to visit him, and inexplicably, he suddenly falls at her feet, clasps her knees, and weeps. Dostoyevsky's description of the event is important: "How it happened he did not know. . . . All at once something seemed to seize him and fling him at her feet. . . . A light of infinite happiness came into her eyes. . . . At last the moment had come."

Note that Rodya *is raised;* he does not raise/resurrect himself. Just as Lazarus was raised from the dead without any volitional act on his own part, so Rodya is raised from sin into new life through the gift of grace. This is not merely a response to human love, although Sonya's love is remarkable; this is a response to divine love. The author then describes the transformation that takes place: "They tried to speak, but they could not. Tears stood in their eyes. They were both pale and thin, but in their white sick faces there glowed the dawn of a new future, a perfect resurrection into a new life. Love had raised them from the dead, and the heart of each held endless springs of life for the heart of the other."

Dostoyevsky goes on to tell us, "Life had taken the place of logic and something quite different must be worked out in his mind." That is yet another major theme for him—life is bigger than mere logic; there is a mystery and a profundity to it. Following his description of Rodya's resurrection, the author writes, "There was a New Testament under his pillow. Mechanically he took it out. It was hers, the very one from which she had read to him the raising of Lazarus to him.

At first he was afraid she would worry him about religion, would talk about the gospel and pester him with books. But to his great surprise she had not once approached the subject and had not even offered him the Testament. He had asked her for it himself. . . . Till now he had not opened it."

Why had Sonya not "pestered" him with religion and books? It seems to be Dostoyevsky's way of showing that she, like Christ, gave herself to him. The testament contained the law, which man could not keep, and it revealed the promise of salvation, but grace came in the person of Christ. The text concludes by saying,

> At the dawn of their happiness, both had been ready, for some moments, to think of those seven years as if they were no more than seven days. He did not even know that the new life would not be his for nothing that it must be dearly bought and paid for with great and heroic struggles yet to come. But that is the beginning of a new story, the story of the gradual renewal of a man, of his gradual regeneration, of his slow progress from one world to another, of how he learned to know of a hitherto undreamed-of reality. All that might be the subject of a new tale, but our present one is ended.

So, we see that this is really a wisdom tale. Indeed, what we have in this novel is a kind of Promethean myth—a revolt and quest for freedom from God. Yet it is a distinctively Christian anthropology that does not permit us to deceive ourselves in supposing that we are basically good. We cannot minimize the reality that Dostoyevsky was a Christian novelist; if one reads his work in that context, it is impossible to argue that faith and religion don't occupy a central role in all his novels, in all his themes and purposes. If readers come from different worldviews and try to understand this novel, they will invariably reduce it to less than the author intended it to be and, in doing so, eliminate the transcendent aspects of the work. Consequently, for such people, the epilogue often appears as mere wishful escapism; many claim it to be the author's weak attempt at a last-minute happy ending. What these assessments fail to grasp, however, is that the gospel is central to the novel's plot long before the epilogue. We see that Sonya is provided as a Christ figure and that like him, she abdicates her own self-will and lives to serve other people.

Indeed, freedom cannot be obtained by the quest for freedom as an end in itself. In the majority of the novel, Raskolnikov was trapped; he had nowhere to turn. Ultimately, Dostoyevsky forces the reader to face the futility of self-will. The attempt to deify the will actually leads to the bondage of the will; it leads to nihilism and hopelessness. It is only those who yield their wills to Christ who gain true freedom and thereby enjoy fellowship with others. Paradoxically, we learn that we can only find life by actually losing it and finding it anew in Christ.

This is a soul-forming world, and we are not here just for comfort. As followers of Jesus, we are being prepared, trained, and developed for eternity. Dostoyevsky's novel provides a reminder that in the power of Christ, our love and service to other people can have a reverberating impact for eternity.

Lord of all things true, good, and beautiful, you are the wellspring of hope, purpose, and meaning. In Jesus you transmute mortality and alienation into the joy of unbounded relational life. In Christ, suffering becomes redemptive and meaningful. May I embrace the true vitality of losing my life and finding it anew in your life.

NOTES

BLAISE PASCAL

Pensées

Introduction

Blaise Pascal was a French mathematician and philosopher of the seventeenth century. He lived from 1623 to 1662, and for most of his adult life, he struggled with chronic illness. In fact, it has been said that from the age of eighteen until his death at age thirty-nine, he did not experience a day without intense pain. Despite this debilitation, however, Pascal's contributions to the intellectual realm are significant.

Pascal's father, Étienne Pascal, viewed education in a rather unconventional way and chose to educate his son at home. Ironically, he did not want Blaise to begin studying mathematics until he was fifteen years old; Étienne even removed all math-related textbooks from the home so that his young son would have no access to independent study of math. Despite these restrictions, the curious Blaise began exploring geometry at age twelve. Without guidance he discovered that the sum of the angles of a triangle are two right angles; this discovery prompted his father to permit him to begin the study of math a bit earlier than age fifteen. He relented and gave him a book on Euclidean theory, and he also began taking the boy with him to meetings he attended with other religious academics. By age sixteen Pascal had already developed several geometry theorems, including one pertaining to the hexagon.

When he was about nineteen, Pascal invented the first digital calculator (in the sense that it calculated digits mechanically). His father was employed as a tax collector for their region of France, and the calculator was designed to assist him in his work. It took him three years to perfect his concept, but the mid-twentieth-century models applied the same basic principles he developed in the mid-seventeenth century.

While in his early twenties, Pascal began experimentation with atmospheric pressure, and it was during this time that he introduced the mathematical concept of the vacuum. Descartes, another leading French mathematician, condemned Pascal's vacuum theory, writing in a letter that "[Pascal] has too much vacuum in his head." Other scientists and mathematicians joined Descartes in his skepticism about the vacuum theory, although Pascal himself remained convinced of its legitimacy. He even wrote in length about it in a work titled *New Experiments Concerning Vacuums.*

Pascal skillfully balanced a life of contemplative thought with academic endeavor. He studied conical structure, triangles, probabilities, calculus, cycloids, and other innovative math concepts. Yet his life took a profound turn when he became a Christian in 1654, at the age of thirty-one. Characteristically, he applied his daunting intellect as passionately to issues of faith as he had to issues of science. He began writing *Pensées* (which translates as "thoughts") in 1656, and his assertions about God are both articulate and logical. He developed a concept that has since been termed "Pascal's wager," where he applied probability to matters of faith, saying, "If God does not exist, one will lose nothing by believing in him, while if he does exist, one will lose everything by not believing. . . . We are compelled to gamble." Pascal also applied his vacuum concept to his faith. He famously wrote of the abyss within every human soul that only God can fill. By this obvious analogy to his vacuum concept, he acknowledged that the soul was created to exist in relationship with God, and apart from that relationship, there remains a void nothing else can fill.

In exploring the life and contributions of Pascal, I am going to rely on three books, particularly one compiled by Os Guinness—an outline of sorts that tries to structure *Pensées* in a reasonably organized form. The problem that we face is that we really don't know precisely what Pascal intended to do with these thoughts. He actually never completed what he was intending to call *Apologetics for the Christian Faith* because he died at age thirty-nine from a stomach tumor that metastasized to his brain. So we have to guess as to what sequence it might have taken when complete. I will also be using a book called *The Mind on Fire*, which contains introductory material by Jim Houston and Os Guinness, as well as a third book, by Peter Kreeft, called *Christianity for Modern Pagans.* Kreeft, a Catholic philosopher, takes some of the key *pensées* and adds some of his own thoughts to them, and his insights are very helpful. He also arranged them according to topic, making Pascal's ponderings highly readable. Kreeft said of his book that it was "not just a book *about* Pascal or an editing *of* Pascal." Neither was it "an 'explanation' of Pascal. Pascal needs no explanations. Rather, it is a *festooning* of Pascal, like decorating a Christmas tree" (preface to *Christianity for Modern Pagans*, italics original). I hope that will also be the nature of this little chapter, as well.

Pensées is a book that, in my opinion, was about 350 years ahead of its time. It might actually be called the first postmedieval apologetic. In it Pascal anticipates the kind of desires for diversion, distraction, and indifference that so fully characterize the twenty-first century—the boredom, apathy, and futility that so many experience. Ironically, *boredom* is a word that did not exist until recently. There was no such word in the medieval or Enlightenment eras. We moderns had to invent the word. Our modern term encompasses previous concepts of *acedia*, *malaise*, and *ennui*—words that communicate an existential kind of *angst*, which, by the way, is a German word connoting the human condition as an existence of pain and ambiguity. Pascal clearly anticipates the inherent struggles if we attempt to live alienated from God, arguing that those very struggles are intended to be used by him to drive us to him.

Pensées, as I have mentioned, is a collection of hundreds of thoughts. Pascal's conviction was that a true and informed Christian apologetic would speak to the human condition through both faith and reason to the whole of our experience. In this work he explores the mind, will, and emotions, as well as concepts from history, science, Scripture, theology, philosophy, and poetry. All these pursuits are brought together in these snippets that evidently were written out on long sheets of paper, thought by thought, over the last years of Pascal's life, from 1657 to 1662.

What he apparently did was draw short lines in between each thought. Then he cut those pages according to each concept and organized them into bundles—twenty-eight bundles to be precise—which he then literally tied together with thread. These bundles were found by the executers of his estate after his death in 1662. Two copies were made, and our modern editions are based on those. A problem, however, is that they were numbered in a way that really wasn't very helpful. So, more recently, admirers of Pascal have attempted to apply some structure and unity to Pascal's writings, to make them more reader friendly. Despite a lack of organizational unity, there remains something powerful about Pascal's aphorisms and idioms. They are unpolished and unfinished, yet they pack a punch; they are characterized by a unique terseness and vividness. Few authors, I think, have captured the human predicament with such clarity, force, power, and passion. Pascal combines a remarkable mind with a tender, seeking heart that is, I think, nearly unparalleled. He is also one of the most ecumenical of the Christian writers, perhaps second only to Augustine, on whom Pascal was highly dependent. Augustine (and more recently C. S. Lewis) is a superb example of an individual whose writings transcend the barriers between Catholicism and Protestantism and who presents cogent and clear visions of "mere Christianity"—the essentials of the Christian faith.

Pascal, as I said, was born in 1623, and his life was a short and intense burst of flame. From the beginning, it was evident that he was quite precocious. He was curious and learned quickly. His mother died when he was only three, so he was raised by his sisters and father. His father, a successful attorney, converted in 1646 to a religious movement termed Jansenism. It was named for its most public proponent, Cornelius Jansen, a Dutch Catholic and bishop of Ypres. Jansen was a staunch Augustinian who in response to the Counter-Reformation of the Catholic Church taught the total depravity of man, the necessity of grace, the sufficiency of Christ, and the absolute sovereignty of God, even over matters of the will and salvation. Jansen was vehemently opposed by the Jesuits, a branch of Catholicism known for its promotion of a faith-plus-works salvation. Among orthodox Catholics, *Jansenism* was a pejorative term; in fact, it was Jesuits who introduced the term in an attempt to discredit Jansen himself.

Although one of Pascal's sisters and his father were known Jansenists, Pascal was not. This is why I deem him so ecumenical; throughout his work, his theology is decidedly Christocentric rather than denominational. He remained a staunch Catholic yet sought to understand biblical truth deeply and accurately.

I think this independence of thought gave him a boldness because he was a man who was not bound by the conventions and convictions of his own culture, and this led to his greatest contribution, which, in my view, was his

Christian literature. Many years ago, Alan Bloom, the late Yale professor, wrote a provocative book titled *The Closing of the American Mind*. In that book he made a very interesting observation related to Pascal. He noted that Alexis de Tocqueville, a nineteenth-century Frenchman who analyzed and wrote about the "American Experiment," had asserted that even today, many people can be divided into two basic camps of thought: *Pascalian* or *Cartesian*. He explains that this is because "Decartes and Pascal represent a choice between reason and revelation, science and piety, the choice from which everything else follows" ("The Clean Slate," *The Closing of the American Mind*). Now Bloom was not a Christian, so his "either/or" option is one we would not fully accept, since the same God is the source of *both* reason and revelation. Yet he makes an important point nevertheless. If we reject the existence of any truth beyond ourselves and adopt the naturalist's view, it alters everything. Likewise, if we acknowledge a created order and an absolute source of all knowledge, it, too, must necessarily alter everything—all views, adherences, and behavior. Pascal understood this, and his writings reflect that understanding.

Although Pascal had a kind of first conversion when he was twenty-three years old, he had a second conversion, a powerful experience, in 1654 at the age of thirty-one. Reflecting on that conversion, he wrote what he called the Memorial. It seems that this spiritual awakening was so powerful that he actually described it on parchment and sewed it in his doublet; every time he would replace his jacket or doublet, he would resew the memorial into its lining. He carried it everywhere he went, and it was found in his jacket following his death. Pascal's memorial read, "Year of Grace 1654. Monday, 23rd November, feast of St. Clement, pope and martyr, and others in the martyrology. Vigil of St. Chrysogonus, martyr, and others. From about half past ten at night until about half past midnight, FIRE. God of Abraham, God of Isaac, God of Jacob, not the God of philosophers and scholars." He then went on to write,

> Certitude. Feeling. Joy. Peace. God of Jesus Christ. My God and your God. Your God shall be my God. Forgetfulness of the world and of everything, except God. He is only found by the ways taught in the Gospels. Grandeur of the human soul. Righteous Father, the world has not known you, but I have known you. Joy, joy, joy, tears of joy. I have departed from him: They have forsaken me, the fount of living water. My God, will you leave me? Let me not be separated from him forever. This is the eternal life, that they know you, the one true God, and the one you sent, Jesus Christ. Jesus Christ. Jesus Christ. I left him; I fled him, renounced, crucified. Let me never be separated from him. He is only kept by the ways taught in the Gospels: renunciation, total and sweet. Complete submission to Jesus Christ and to my director. Eternally in joy for a day's striving on the earth. I will not forget your words. Amen.

That is what he carried with him everywhere, and yet no one knew about it. Pascal did not tell anyone of this experience, and it was only after his death that the impact of this powerful two-hour encounter with the living God became known. It transformed his life.

That night of fire became so decisive for the remaining eight years of his life that it altered his whole course. It spurred him to write his *Provincial Letters*, theological statements that satirized the Jesuit attacks against Jansenism and offered a Christ-centered response to the religious controversy. Originally, he wrote these letters anonymously because it was quite dangerous to challenge the views of the powerful Jesuits. These letters eventually became classics of French satirical literature. In fact, Voltaire regarded Pascal as one of the finest French prose writers. Of course, Voltaire also regarded him as very dangerous in his religious views, for they were antithetical to those held by Voltaire himself.

Pascal's gift was in his ability to appeal not only to the mind but also to the heart. He possessed not only a clear and trenchant mind but also an equally passionate heart. It is this unique combination that makes him so relevant today. In fact, he is better known and perhaps more revered today than he was a century ago and definitely more now than in his own lifetime. His writing speaks to us in a timeless way.

Pascal's Aphorisms

Pascal's famous aphorisms are often quoted. One of the best known of these may be his statement that "the heart has its reasons, of which reason knows nothing." With this statement, he acknowledged the inherent limitations of reason to fully explain matters of faith. He also asserted in another aphorism that "if man were happy, the less he were diverted the happier he would be." He understood that distraction is a symptom *of* unhappiness, not a means *to* happiness. Pascal further observed, "The sole cause for man's unhappiness is that he does not know how to stay quietly in his room." How true this is of our modern world. We are uncomfortable with silence and solitude, for it forces us to face ourselves and the reality of the human condition.

These sample aphorisms illustrate the fact that the writings of Pascal are not linear but cumulative. He builds on previous concepts, and he goes back and forth between them. He communicates with a powerful terseness and clarity about human misery and how misery plays a role in awakening awareness of the human condition. He asserts that distraction is an attempt at escapism—an attempt to avoid dealing with the difficult questions of life.

He also deals with common fallacies, including our tendency to pit one extreme against the other in a narrow either/or option. People view themselves as caught between the finite and the infinite, between misery and grandeur, between reason and the heart, between reason and authority. Many people feel trapped by these seemingly oppositional pulls. Pascal then illustrates a third option, namely, the gospel. He provides an apologetic that asserts the reality that humanity, though fallen, is redeemable through the atoning work of Jesus Christ. He is highly Christocentric; everything in his thought and writing ultimately converges on the person and the work of Jesus Christ. At one point he wrote, "Jesus Christ is the object of all things and the center toward which all things tend." His synthesis of reason and faith is evident in that declaration.

In Pascal, we have a man whose intellectual integrity, as Os Guinness writes, "is matched perfectly by his lonely courage in suffering and by the ardor for his love for God." When he had his powerful vision in 1654, he was seized by a certitude—an assurance, not just a probability—of the reality of the God of Abraham, Isaac, and Jacob. He grasped the presence of a God who is personal, palpable, and intensely real.

As a result, he also grasped the grandeur of the human soul juxtaposed with its fallenness—humanity's glory and depravity. When he embraced God's offer of grace through faith, Pascal was able to see reason in its proper context. In the final years of his life, he began to challenge the reductionism of the rationalism advocated in the writings of his peers, such as Montaigne. He saw that they attempted to unify their worldview solely through human reason, and yet in doing so, they reduced everything to something smaller, lacking both vitality and reality. Commenting on this problem, Pascal observed, "The misery of Man is that he is lost and he can not find the appropriate ways of knowing simply by the ways of using his intellect." There is a dialectical tension in his work as he establishes the necessity of faith in order to see beyond the limitations of reason itself.

He then traces God's sure and certain work in human history. He looks at the history of Israel, the fulfillment of general and messianic prophecies, and the evidences of the resurrection. He then poses a proposition that he calls the wager, where he says, "You don't have a choice not to choose." In other words, to fail to choose is itself a choice.

And so he says, "It would be prudent to wager carefully and properly because the implications are not trivial." He clarifies the nature of such a choice, saying, "The final step that is needful is volitional. It is not merely a cognitive assent but there is a volitional apprehension and reception." Pascal relied heavily on Augustinian theology; therefore, he recognized the profound need for grace. Like Augustine, he believed that the will is effectively under bondage until God's grace intervenes. He saw the mystery of that tension but said, "Our need is to humbly accept and to receive the grace of the living God."

Now Pascal, as I said earlier, suffered terribly throughout his life, but he prayed diligently for God to use his sickness for his own glory. Here is one of those prayers: "With perfect consistency of mind help me to receive all manner of events. For we know not what to ask and we cannot ask for one event rather than another without presumption. We cannot desire a specific action without presuming to be a judge and assuming responsibility for what, in your wisdom, you may hide from me. Lord, I know only one thing, that it is good to follow you and wicked to offend you. Beyond this I do not know what is good for me."

Pascal was right. We do not know what our best interests look like. He continues, "I do not know what is good for me, whether health or sickness, riches or poverty, or anything else in this world. This knowledge surpasses both the wisdom of men and the wisdom of angels. It lies hidden in the secrets of your providence, which I adore and will not dare to pry open." This is a daring and bold prayer because it requires radical and absolute surrender to the providence of the living

God, a childlike trust in God's goodness and purposes.

In asking that God would use the tension within his own life to help him grow in trust and humility, Pascal renounced a great deal. He renounced marriage. He renounced property. He renounced money, intellect, and the smug sovereignty of his own self-will. He also practiced some rather extreme forms of external asceticism, which I would not encourage any of us to pursue. For instance, he would not receive friends unless he was wearing an inner garment that pressed small studded nails against his flesh. He was, therefore, always in physical pain when he was with his friends; he believed this prevented him from enjoying those friendships excessively and therefore kept him from being pulled away from God to the things of this world. Obviously, nowhere in Scripture does God demand such self-abuse. In fact, fellowship is a quality of the Trinity and a gift from God. There is wonderful joy in human companionship. Yet even though Pascal practiced some misguided asceticism, he clearly conveyed a remarkable grasp of truth on many other levels.

Pascal rose above his own age. He lived a life of what we might call daring, intellectual loneliness. He was a hero-saint whose intense life made a profound difference to others. His thoughts, his *Pensées*, are alive. They are like bolts of lightning. Even as he was writing them, he saw that the years were short. He was literally fighting against time. Additionally, he fought increasing physical pain, depression, and weakness, realizing that each day could be his last. Through his writing, then, he lived in light of eternity. It is my own conviction that God, in his sovereignty, let this saint burn out before the work was complete so that there would be an enduring passion and relevance, a force and intensity and sense of urgency in his writing. *Pensées* is a book that I am convinced will be in print until Christ Jesus returns. Furthermore, it is a book we should read more than once; it ages well. Os Guinness actually said he has made it a practice to read this book every year for thirty years. That is saying a good deal. I must say, every time I read it, I always get something more out of it. That is one of the tests of a great classic.

In commenting on *Pensées*, Peter Kreeft put it this way: "This book, if you wanted to use the great ideals of style and of life itself, the true, the good and the beautiful, what words would we use?" He continues, "Pascal is lyrical, eloquent, delicate yet potent, witty, gem-like, incisive, stunning, biting, provocative, arresting, sharp, haunting, even terrifying. But, he also writes that which is true. He is precise. He is rigorous. He is accurate, objective, concrete, empirical, enlightening, scientific, brilliant, wise and intelligent. But, not only did he write that which was beautiful, and that which was true, he also wrote that which was good. Words to describe that would be warm, and personal, and passionate, and intimate, and loving, and tender, and heartening, curative and disarming, earnest, all of that, which is good."

In *Pensées* Pascal makes this observation, "We are caught between the finite and the infinite." We see in this constant movement between one extreme and the other this balancing act that he plays on in his writing. "These dualisms," he says, "are not ultimate but rather they are relative in the human condition." There is a dialectic of the contradictions that he described that can only be resolved by a third truth that cannot be attained through deduction or empirical analysis. That third truth requires the grace of revelation. Only that will take those half-truths and reveal something greater—not a human synthesis, but rather the synthesis of revelation that helps us understand the fundamental questions we all must ask: (1) the question of origin: Where did I come from? (2) the question of purpose: Why am I here? and (3) the question of destiny: Where am I going? Those three questions cannot be adequately answered by human philosophy. Revelation offers the only ultimate answer to them.

Overview

Let me now transition to the writings themselves. The book I mentioned earlier, *The Mind on Fire,* seeks to reconstruct how Pascal might have intended his packets of ponderings to be presented. It suggests three divisions, and I think that structure makes some sense. First, Pascal addresses the misery of man—of the human condition—without God. Many of his thoughts deal with man's natural condition, his unhappy condition, man's attempts to rationalize behavior and attitudes, and the contradiction between man's potential greatness and the inconsistency that characterizes reality. Pascal also deals with a second topic in his writing: the significance of and limitations of human reason. A third theme that can be found is that God has reached down into our lives, revealing himself, his love, and his plan of redemption.

Let's begin by exploring that first section about the human condition without God. Pascal says—and this is one of his best-known *pensées*—"Man is merely a reed. The weakest thing in nature, but he is a thinking reed." With this statement, he acknowledges a very important distinction between man and everything else in the created order. Yet he ironically notes his fragility and vulnerability when he says, "There is no need for the whole universe to take up arms and crush him, a vapor or a drop of water is enough to kill him." With these thoughts, he introduces one of the primary dilemmas of life: How do we reconcile man's greatness with his finiteness?

He goes on to say, "Though the universe were to crush him, Man would still be nobler than his destroyer because he is dying and knows the universe has the advantage over him but the universe knows nothing of this." In other words, it is our dignity that causes us to be aware of the reality of death. Look at cattle. They are being moved into the pen for death, and they watch one animal after another go to its death, yet remain unaware of the impending threat. But man is acutely aware of death. This is the topic of the greatest plays, poems, and novels generated by the human mind. Hamlet agonizingly asks, "What is this quintessence of man?" and "What is a man, if his chief good . . . be but to sleep and feed?" Hemingway's "old man" declares that man is not made for defeat even as he observes its inevitability. Burns declares that the field mouse, facing imminent starvation and death, enjoys a preferable existence to man because "the present only touches thee [the mouse]: / But oh! I backward cast my e'e / On prospects drear! / An' forward tho' I cannot see, / I guess an' fear!" (from *To a Mouse*). Blake, too, observes something very similar when he writes, "If thought is life / And strength and breath, / And the want of thought is death; / Then am I / A happy fly, / If I live or if I die" (from *The Fly*). What struggle did each of these brilliant minds face? Simply this: How do we begin to reconcile man's awareness and aspirations with the inevitability of death?

The fact is that we are aware of its imminence. We are aware of the passage of time. "What kind of freak is man," Pascal says in another thought; "What a novelty he is, how absurd he is, how chaotic and what a mass of contradictions and yet what a prodigy. He is judge of all things and yet a feeble worm. He is repository of truth and yet sinks into such doubt and error. He is the glory and the scum of the universe." Strong words those. He does not mince his words, and for good reason; he wants to grip his reader's attention. He wants to force us to think, whether we like it or not. He observes the immensity of the cosmos and notes that man is a cosmic blip, in effect. But, then he says, on the other hand, "We ourselves, our bodies, are like universes." If you compare the body to something very tiny, it would be like a universe, a cosmos. We find ourselves in the middle of these two infinities, these two abysses.

He looks at a simple little creature, such as a mite, and he talks about and marvels at its economy of size and that it is so complete; its little joints and organs are all in place, and they work. Frankly, even a mite is a marvel. We are far from creating such a thing. With nuclear magnetic resonance and x-ray crystallography, our capacity to discern these microscopic life-forms has caused us to realize they are a lot more impressive than we had previously guessed. Intelligent design, irreducible complexity—once again I believe Pascal would have been on the cutting edge of that understanding if he were alive today. He then observes, "As to ourselves, this is the thing we understand least. Man is the greatest prodigy in nature. We can not conceive what body is, and still less what mind is."

When I was a little boy, I recall watching a television show where some fellow had committed an act of violence and was wandering in the woods. I was confused, so I asked my parents what he was doing. They responded by saying that he had lost his mind, but their explanation meant little to a six-year-old. I tried to imagine what kind of a mind the man was looking for? I had only an abstract concept that he was looking for something important in the woods and was unable to find it. Sometimes I think I have no better idea what that mind is now than I did when I was six. It remains deeply mysterious. How does it relate to the body? Why is the human mind unique among living creatures? That is a whole source of philosophical debate that has yet to be satisfactorily resolved. Pascal continues, "The way in which minds are attached to bodies is beyond Man's understanding and yet this is what Man is."

He then discusses the human condition of boredom. "A definition of Man," he says, "is of a being of dependence longing for independence and having needs." That is an apt definition. Each of us is a contradiction, and we cannot escape from our own dilemma. This is a facet of the existential dilemma.

"The characteristic of human nature," Pascal says, "is to love oneself and to consider only oneself. But what else can it do? It cannot help its own love, being inconsistent and miserable. It wants to be great and sees itself as only small. It wants to be happy and finds that it is wretched. It wants to be perfect and sees itself full of imperfections. It wants to be the object of other people's love and esteem and sees that its faults deserve only its dislike and contempt." That is why, as Samuel Johnson put it, "every man has that in himself that he dare not tell his dearest friend." Everyone is terrified of exposure; the trauma of transparency is a frightening thing. Yet Pascal also says, "Nothing is of more importance to Man than his state; nothing more fearful than eternity. It is unnatural that there should be people who are indifferent to the loss of their life and careless of the peril of an eternity of unhappiness. They react very differently to everything else. They are afraid of the least things that they anticipate and feel. The same person who spends nights and days in rage and in the agony of despair over the loss of some status or imaginary affront is the same person who knows he will lose everything by death and shows neither concern or emotion at the prospect."

Why is it that we are consumed with trivial and petty affronts and yet know we are going to lose everything when we die? We obsess on the trivial. A perplexed Pascal writes, "It is extraordinary to see in the same heart and at the same time this concern for the most trivial matters and yet lack of concern for the greatest." This is the tension that we live in daily. And so Pascal says, "We have become adept at diversion. All our life passes this way. We seek rest by struggling against certain obstacles and once they are overcome, rest proves intolerable because of the boredom it produces. We must get away from it and crave excitement."

It is true that we often identify ourselves by one activity after another. A friend of mine has a remote cabin in the mountains of North Carolina; it is quietly tucked away. Once he invited some people to come and stay with him at his cabin. They in turn asked him for a list of activities they could do while they were there, but he didn't have anything for them to do. They immediately asked, "What do you do when you are there?" This amused my friend, for although there were no remarkable activities, there were a thousand things to enjoy, among them, the escape from hurry and stress.

Along these same lines, how many of us have come back from a vacation wearier than when we left? Pascal notes, "Man is so unhappy that he would be bored even if he had no cause for boredom. By the very nature of his temperament he is so vain; though he has a thousand basic reasons for being bored the slightest thing like pushing a ball with a billiard cue will be enough to divert him." He then offers a gambling analogy: "A given man lives life free from boredom by gambling a small sum every day. Give him the money he might win that day, but on the condition that he does not gamble, and you will make him unhappy. It might be argued that what he wants is the entertainment of gaming and not the winnings. Make him play, then, for nothing. His interest will not be fired and he will become bored."

Pascal then asserts, "He must have excitement. He must delude himself into imagining he would be happy to win what he would not want as a gift, if it meant giving up gambling." He analyzes this with one practical illustration after another of the bizarre condition that is the human condition. "Surely it is a development of spectacular social significance," Peter Kreeft writes, "that the very thing ancient saints and sages loved and longed for is the thing we imposed on our most desperate criminals as the cruelest torture our mind can devise: solitude."

Indifference is yet another stratagem by which we attempt to deal with the existential dilemma. We might well say that indifference is the opposite of love. It is further from the love of God than the hatred of God. Isn't it true that you can love a person and hate a person at the same time? We all know what that is like, and yet we cannot love and be indifferent to a person at the same time. Indifference is another matter entirely. "Let us," Pascal says, "examine our thoughts and we will find them wholly concerned with the past or the future. We almost never think of the present." Pascal writes, "And if we do think of it, it is only to see what light it throws on our plans for the future. The present is never our end. The past and the present are our means; the future alone is our end. Thus, we never actually live, but hope to live and since we are always planning how to be happy, it is inevitable that we should never be so."

He is effectively saying that we tend to live either in the past or in the future, but we are rarely alive to this thing that is called "the now." Yet all we have is this now. Martyred missionary Jim Elliot once said, "Wherever you are, be all there." C. S. Lewis also warned of this struggle with time in his *Screwtape Letters* when he wrote, "Biological necessity makes all [man's] passions point in that direction [future] already, so that thought about the Future inflames hope and fear. . . . In a word, the future is, of all things, the thing *least like* eternity. It is the most completely temporal part of time—for the past is frozen and no longer flows, and the present is all lit up with eternal rays. . . . Hence nearly all vices are rooted in the

Future. Gratitude looks to the Past and love to the Present; fear, avarice, lust, and ambition look ahead."

What does he mean? Only that the primary sphere in which God works in temporal man is the present, and so the temptation becomes to live in some other, less useful sphere. How many people live in the regret or nostalgia of the past or in the fear or longing for the future. Instead, we are called to live to the hilt in the present, in accordance with the revealed will of God. It is a very insightful comment. It is very hard for us to live in the now.

Walker Percy, in his novel *The Second Coming,* puts it this way: "He went through his life never really active, never really alive in the present now." He then asks, "Is it possible for someone to miss his life the way someone misses a train?" Sadly, the answer is yes; it clearly is possible. How many people have lived in the future all their lives, pinning their hopes on some anticipated achievement and becoming trapped in the mindset of believing "If I only get this" or "When I get that I'll be happy"? Then they finally reach the point where they must admit, against their desire, that they don't have much more ahead. That is when they start living in the past. And thus at the end of their journey, they find that they have never really lived.

Pascal says such error is a matter of diversion, of distraction or indifference, and powerfully dangerous. He goes on to say, "All look for happiness without exception. Although they use different means they all strive toward this objective. This is why some go to war and some do other things. This is the motive behind every deed of Man, including those who hang themselves." Even with that desperate act, the person is attempting a pursuit of a sort of distorted happiness by trying to avoid the pain of a miserable existence. And so Pascal goes on to say, "He vainly searches but finds nothing to help him other than to see an infinite abyss that can only be filled by one who is infinite and immutable." In other words, there is a boundless void that can be filled only by God himself.

There is a popular misconception that Pascal penned the famous quote, "There is a God-shaped vacuum in every human heart." What he actually said was, "There is an infinite abyss that can only be filled by God Himself." I don't know who came up with the former phrase, but it is not found in Pascal's writings. It is a modernized interpretation of his original one, although an accurate one, we might add. The fact is that we see in human nature, in our desires, and in our human condition a wild variety of aspirations, of pulls, of longings, but none of them satisfy our hearts. To allude to seventeenth-century poet George Herbert in his poem "The Pulley," we attempt to fill our emptiness with God's good gifts while, in a horrible irony, only God himself can satisfy that longing.

Pascal actually sets up a case to describe the human condition so he can talk about God's divine initiative and provision for the human condition. He talks in terms, as I said earlier, of volition. He says, "There are only three kinds of people: Those who have found God and serve Him. Those who are busy seeking God but have not yet found Him. And those who spend their lives neither seeking Him nor finding Him." He says, "The first are reasonable and happy. The last are foolish and unhappy. The middle group are unhappy but reasonable." I would argue that volition, this *seeking*, is really an act of the will and that it is a moral choice as a consequence. We need to seek. That is the distinction. "The absolute distinction between the heavenly and the hellish is not between believers and unbelievers," as Peter Kreeft writes, but "between seekers and non-seekers."

Listen to these words because they are very important. Kreeft says, "All unbelievers who seek will eventually become believers who find, according to the very highest authority. [Matthew 7:7–8: 'For everyone who asks receives, and he who seeks finds, and to him who knocks it will be opened.'] The distinction between believers and seeking unbelievers is only temporary; but the distinction between seeking unbelievers and unseeking unbelievers is eternal." The reality is that there is a great deal more difference between those who seek and those who do not seek than those who have found and those who have not yet found. Kreeft continues, "The great divide, then, is not between theists and atheists or between happiness and unhappiness but between seekers or lovers and non-seekers or non-lovers of truth, for God is truth." It is the heart and not the head that determines destiny.

So, the fundamental question is whom or what do you seek? That is the first question that Jesus Christ asked in John 1:38. When the disciples approached Jesus, his question was, "What do you seek?" I would argue that the answer to that question will determine a person's life, destiny, and, in fact, everything. What we seek will define us. Kreeft notes, "If we do not love the truth, we will not seek it. If we do not seek it, we will not find it. If we do not find it, we will not know it. And if we do not know it we have failed our fundamental task in time and also in eternity."

Pascal comments in this way: "There is always enough light to illuminate the elect and enough obscurity to humble them. There is enough obscurity to blind the reprobate and enough light to condemn them and deprive them of any excuse." He says, "God has ordered nature and reality in such a way that those who choose not to know can find an excuse for not knowing. Those who choose to know will find credible reason for doing so. The heart has its reasons, which reason does not know, but reason, still, is not inimical to the heart." They are not at odds or at loggerheads.

"You are not a free agent," Pascal says. "You are committed to making a choice." Here he again employs the image of a gambler and says, "How will you bet?" He then offers a hypothetical situation: "Let us assess two situations. If you bet on God's existence," and he means more than just an intellectual bet, "if you win, you win everything. But if you lose, you lose nothing. Don't hesitate but take the bet that he exists." Here is what he means: If God does not exist, and you bet that he does, what did you lose? You didn't lose anything. If we are truly alone in the universe, then it is inevitable that we are going to become cosmic blips and be annihilated. If God doesn't exist but you think he does, it may give you the sense of a more meaningful life now, although you are deluded. Frankly, you don't lose much in the long run. But suppose you bet that God doesn't exist? Suppose you choose not to seek him, and in fact it turns out to your horror that he does? You lose everything. That is *Pascal's wager*.

The fact is that what God offers is not merely a bet but a proposal of marriage. God has proposed to us. When a man is standing at the altar and he is asked, "Will you have this woman to be your lawfully wedded wife," he does not respond by saying, "I do believe that she will make a wonderful companion" or "I think she would be a great cook and a great mother of our children." Those are not the appropriate or desired answers. The anticipated answer reflects the man's willingness to take the plunge of commitment—the covenant words "I will." God's offer is perpetually extended to us, his intended bride, but at the end of the day, it is a volitional issue that defines us. We are, as I have said, the product of our choices, and those choices are the product of our aspirations—of that which we seek and of that which we pursue.

Peter Kreeft makes a remarkably relevant statement. He says, "One wonders how much of Christianity's power to win the world has been crippled by the modern fashion of denying or ignoring the reality of Hell. It is certainly a fashion rather than a proof or a discovery." Nothing new came along to change the rules. It became simply a spirit of our time. He says, "Both reason and faith inform us of Hell. Reason because it is irrational to think that souls created free to refuse God can be compelled to accept Him." Suppose a person says that he or she doesn't want to go to heaven, and God says, "You're coming whether you like it or not." What becomes of choice then? To use the marriage analogy again, marriage involves a willingness—a volitional agreement—to enter into the marriage union. When union occurs without willingness—apart from a volitional agreement—we term that *rape*. God extends his loving invitation, but he does not impose himself on us against our wills. To do otherwise would be to annihilate love.

Kreeft, working from Pascal's thoughts, goes on to say, "If no one goes to Hell, then Jesus is a liar or a fool, for He more than anyone warned of it." Frankly, the power and the punch of the wager have lost its power today because we suppose there is no downside to the choice to pursue nothing. Nondecision agnosticism has been elevated to a virtue, but it is not a virtue. It is to contradict what the heart pursues, what the mind needs, and what the will desires.

And so, I am arguing here that it is really not a question of option. "To know God without knowing our own wretchedness," Pascal writes, "only makes for pride. Knowing our own wretchedness without knowing God only makes for despair. Knowing Jesus Christ provides the balance because He shows us both God and our own wretchedness." We are called to be married to God, united to God, and to share in his own life. Do you see that God is the one who is the lover of our souls? Although we spit in his face, he loves us. So deep, so profound, so awesome is his love that though we seek to turn away, he continues to woo us and to offer his love.

Conclusion

I will conclude with some thoughts from the latter portion of *Pensées* where Pascal finally converges his thoughts in the person and work of Jesus Christ. He says, "The ordinary life of a man is like that of the saints. We all seek satisfaction and they only differ according to the object in which they locate it." He asserts, like Augustine, that ultimately the satisfaction of the human heart is based on relationship with our Creator. As Augustine affirmed in his *Confessions*: "You have made us for yourself, and our hearts are restless until they find their rest in you."

Pascal goes on to say, "Do small things in this world as if they were great." This insight really convicted me. I sometimes struggle with thinking that the small things in life are getting in the way of my ministry and of my effectiveness and that I am nonproductive when I am doing trivial things. I am an intuitive, and I don't like details. Yet life is filled with all sorts of sensory details and problems to be solved. Pascal says, "Do small things as if they were great because of the majesty of Christ, who does them in us and lives on in our life. Do great things as if they were small and easy because of His almighty power." What he is saying is that there is splendor in the ordinary.

While we tend to group our activities into categories of importance, Pascal suggests that anything done to God's glory, through the power of Christ, whether mundane or extraordinary, pleases God and helps the body of Christ. He states, "The slightest movement affects the whole of nature; one stone can alter the whole sea. Likewise, in the realm of grace, the slightest action affects everything because of its consequences; therefore everything matters." Kreeft comments on this observation, adding, "Here is the great principle of solidarity, spiritual and mystical and universal. Every sin harms everyone in the Body, and every act of love and obedience to the Head helps every organ in the Body." With this statement he affirms the significance of all our actions, large or small, when we are part of the body of Christ.

There is another phrase that I have come to love, and it is this: "Love God in all things." In other words, we can love God in our relationships. We can love God in our work. We can choose to love God even in our recreation. If you think about it, we can love God in any activity. There is no sacred-secular distinction when we realize we are doing everything for the sake of the name. All things can connect together. Finally, in his statement number 946, Pascal writes,

> Consider Jesus Christ in every person and in ourselves. Jesus Christ has father in His Father. Jesus Christ has brother in His brothers. Jesus Christ has poor in the poor. Jesus Christ has rich in the rich. Jesus Christ has priest and doctor in priests and doctors. Jesus Christ has sovereign in princes, etc. For by His glory He is everything that is great by being God and by his mortal life He is everything that is wretched and abject. That is why He took on this unhappy condition so that He could be, in every person, a model for every condition of Man.

The fact is, Christ knows what it is like to be rejected, to be betrayed, to suffer indignity, to suffer misunderstanding and abuse, and ultimately to suffer physical cruelty and death because he has suffered in every way that we have suffered. He has been tempted in every way that we have been tempted, yet without sin. This deeply Christocentric concept is also summarized in a profound statement by Pascal: "Not only do we know God through Jesus Christ but we only know ourselves through Jesus Christ. We only know life and death through Jesus Christ. Apart from Jesus Christ we can not know the meaning of our life or of death or of God or of ourselves."

As I conclude, I want to go back to an earlier statement: "The heart has its reasons, which reason does not know." I'd like to offer some applications of this truth. First, I would encourage us to be a people who strive to synthesize mind, heart, and will. Even though our natural disposition is perhaps to be more of a thinker or a feeler or a chooser, the fact is that it is good for us to balance those. If one is a more cognitive kind of person, it is a good thing to exercise the other components. Or, if one is a feeling kind of person, it is a good thing to exercise the mind. Pascal demonstrated a profound connection between all of them.

I would also encourage us to truly live each day in light of the grace of God and to remember that everything we do can be done to the glory of God and the good of others. Productivity is an illusion because we misdefine it. We suppose that the big-splash things are going to be more impressive in the kingdom of God than the little acts of fidelity. But in the economy of the kingdom, those small things can have more power and more meaning, even though they are unsung and unknown, than great achievements found in church history textbooks—fidelity in the small things matters. The Scriptures remind us that "he who is faithful in a very little thing is faithful also in much" and that "he who is unrighteous in a very little thing is unrighteous also in much."

I would also urge all of us to consider the virtue of humility, not as an end in itself, however. The more we reflect on the grace of God, the more we have a foundation for true humility. If we focus on humbling ourselves, we will be focusing only on ourselves. Ironically, it will be a perverse form of pride. So, it is prudent to focus on the grace of God because the more we consider what he has done *for* us, the more we see ourselves in that light.

I would also encourage each of us to be a person who develops a passion for truth, one who sees that truth is not just cognitive but actually has profound heart implications, and who remembers that all truth is God's truth. Finally, I encourage us to be a people who transcend our culture. It is much easier to acquiesce to culture or react to it by becoming provincial. That is why C. S. Lewis, in more than one place, argued that it is a good thing, when we read, to read old books. He recommended, "Read an old book for every new book you read." Or, if you can't do that, at least read one old one for every three new ones. If we do not sink our wells deeply into some of the earlier literature he said, we risk becoming merely a product of our own time and culture—people who merely parrot the opinions of popular culture.

> Father, we thank you for these great and timeless truths, for the marvelous hero-saint that Pascal was and for how he was enflamed by your truth and impassioned for your purposes. May we be the same. May we be a people who

understand that the things that we long for, seek, and desire most will ultimately define us. Let our life quest be always for you. Let our accomplishments be always for your glory. Help us live actively in the present yet to rest confidently in the future as we learn to trust you. We pray these things in Christ's name. Amen.

NOTES

C. S. LEWIS

The Great Divorce

Introduction

A few years ago, there was a remarkable article called "Myth Matters" in the April 23, 2001, issue of *Christianity Today.* It was written by Louis Markos, a C. S. Lewis scholar, who asserted in the article that Christians need to have a more incarnational view of art—one that takes literature seriously. Markos regards C. S. Lewis as a genius at combining logic and imagination, for he had the ability to rigorously present truth while simultaneously stimulating his readers' senses and inspiring in them a childlike wonder and awe. Markos says, "Unlike so many contemporary Christian academics that passively accept the existing assumptions upon which their discipline is based and then meekly ask that God's name be mentioned now and then, Lewis went on the offensive and challenged the assumptions themselves. The pure Lewis tempered his logic with a love for beauty and wonder and magic. His conversion to Christ not only freed his mind from the bonds of a narrow stoicism, it freed his heart to fully embrace his earlier passion for mythology." I agree with Markos when he says, "Modernism has killed nature and soured the universe and the Church has done nothing to restore the cosmos to life."

Here is an irony: in the Middle Ages Christians held a view of the universe as a place teeming with life, meaning, and purpose; but that image has been discarded, a fact that prompted the name of one of Lewis's academic books, *The Discarded Image*. In it, he discusses the unifying view of an ordered universe connected to the cosmos and its inhabitants. Actually, this subject animates much of Lewis's own writing, particularly his fiction. In his space trilogy and The Chronicles of Narnia, the image of God as the unifying personage of the universe is clearly conveyed. Lewis understood what Paul so clearly grasped: "He Himself gives to all people life and breath and all things" (Acts 17:25).

The Markos article dealt with one of Lewis's more important critiques of modernism, which examines the modernist's assumption that higher things are always copies of lower things. For example, Marxism's claim that ideology merely reflects underlying economic forces; Darwin's belief that more complex life-forms, like human beings, evolve from lower, less complex life-forms; Freud's insistence that love and charity are but a sublimation of lust—that sort of a thing.

Lewis called this "nothing-buttery," a term by which he criticized views that argued that what we see as high or unifying is "nothing-but" and merely reflects a temporal world. Lewis's writing challenges that perspective. Much of Lewis's creative and apologetic energy is devoted to demonstrating that lower things are, in fact, copies of higher things. The realm of the eternal is what is real and permanent; our world is a mere shadow. We dwell in the "shadowlands," and our greatest moments of beauty, our greatest moments in relationships, our greatest experiences of aesthetic wonder and adventure are merely hints of reality and, as Lewis elsewhere says, "patches of Godlight on the woodlands of our experience." They are hints of home, but we are not yet home.

Lewis talks about this idea of longing in *Surprised by Joy* as well as in a sermon titled "The Weight of Glory." He notes that sometimes we experience a longing for something but can't quite connect the longing to anything in reality or past experience: "These things—the beauty, the memory of our own past—are good images of what we really desire; but if they are mistaken for the thing itself, they turn into dumb idols, breaking the hearts of their worshippers. For they are not the thing itself; they are only the scent of a flower we have not found, the echo of a tune we have not heard, news from a country we have never visited." But one day we will, he says, find that "the door we have been knocking on all our lives will open at last."

Lewis took fiction very seriously, and Markos's article goes on to explore how he used irony, paradox, and ambiguity as metaphors and symbols of the existence and reality of transcendent truths. Lewis had a way of smuggling Christianity in the back door. Many people have read The

Chronicles of Narnia without ever realizing that the books contain Christian themes, and yet as they meet and grow to love Aslan, they are subtly being introduced to the love of Jesus. There is something powerful about those stories, for they contain pictures of truth.

Background on C. S. Lewis

At this point I would like to interject a brief word about Lewis himself, and I will be alluding to aspects of Kathryn Lindskoog's book *C. S. Lewis: Mere Christian*, which contains some helpful insights. Lindskoog describes Lewis as a man of "mirth, girth and humility," which seems to summarize well his character. Lindskoog relates, "He had a marvelous and magical childhood for nine years until his mother died of cancer. During that time . . . , Clive Lewis and his older brother, Warren, spent an extraordinary amount of time outdoors, drawing, riding, yearning for the distant hills on the horizon."

After their mother's death, however, the brothers were sent off to a nightmarish boarding school in England. It was one of the worst experiences of their young lives. Warren Lewis later described the impact of this experience: "With his uncanny flair for making the wrong decision, my father had given us helpless children into the hands of a madman." Essentially, they were left in a terrible school under the supervision of an incompetent staff. Despite their repeated protestations, their father was convinced they were at an excellent institution and never grasped the damage it inflicted on his boys.

By his mid-teens Lewis had become enamored of mythology, particularly Norse myths, and had also begun to dabble in occultism. By this time he was in a preparatory school, and his relationship with his father was strained. It was during these teen years that he concluded Christianity was merely another mythology and so committed himself to atheism. After preparatory school he attended Malvern College. Although Lewis had a tremendously powerful inner imaginative life, he generally hated his schools. He disliked being forced into sports and other activities. So the library became his place of escape. He adored poetry, medieval romance, and Norse, Celtic, and classical mythology. He later wondered if his adoration of false gods, in whom he did not believe, was the true God's way of developing in him a keen capacity for worship. Lewis always recognized the value of myths, regarding them as bent versions of truth and therefore useful tools in teaching truth. Lewis's good friend J. R. R. Tolkien even asserted that in the incarnation, myth and history became one. He termed this concept the "eucatastrophe," a catastrophic irruption into human history for good. For that is what the incarnation was, the decisive revelation of God in his manifest glory.

When the First World War broke out, Lewis was sent to study with an atheistic tutor, an elderly Scotsman by the name of Kilpatrick, whom Lewis nicknamed the Great Knock since he knocked or challenged everything Lewis said. In fact, he challenged him constantly. Kilpatrick had a high regard for logical argumentation, and therefore he challenged Lewis to think with tremendous intellectual rigor. He wouldn't tolerate any sloppy thought.

This educational experience marked Lewis for life because he learned to write with clarity and precision and at the same time with imagination. During the years he was in the lively environment of Surrey, he bought many books, and one of those books was a copy of *Phantastes*, by George MacDonald. He later claimed that this work baptized his imagination. MacDonald's Christian fantasy made a profound impact on Lewis's thinking; in fact, he even incorporates MacDonald as a guide in *The Great Divorce*. Lewis was also influenced during those developmental years by writer G. K. Chesterton.

After serving in World War I, Lewis studied at Oxford, where he was later offered a position as a lecturer. His religious and philosophical views started to change, and he began to believe that there had to be a mind involved in the universe, but he didn't want this mind to be God. If God were to turn out to be personal, then he would have to answer to him. Even though he became more open to religious ideas, Lewis's conversion did not actually take place until 1929. His account of his conversion is often quoted: "You might picture me, alone in that room at Magdalene [Magdalene was where he was teaching], night after night, for whenever my mind lifted from my work, there was the steady, unrelenting approach of Him whom I so earnestly desired not to meet." Obviously, he wasn't looking for God; he was trying to avoid God's claim on his life. Yet he acknowledges "that which I greatly feared had at last come upon me in the Trinity term [spring] of 1929 and I gave in and admitted that God was God, knelt and prayed, perhaps that night the most dejected and reluctant convert in all of England."

As he puts it, he "went kicking and screaming into the kingdom." But, that still wasn't his full conversion. That didn't happen until 1931. For almost two years he struggled against believing that Jesus was God, in part because he thought the incarnation would bring God nearer in yet another way. It was two Christian friends, J. R. R. Tolkien and Hugo Dyson, who influenced him in this final stage of his conversion.

His autobiography, *Surprised by Joy,* relates his rather unusual experience of coming to know Christ as Savior. On a sunny morning in 1931, at the age of thirty-three, he was riding to the Whipsnade Zoo in the sidecar of his brother Warren's motorcycle. He recalled, "When we set out I did not believe that Jesus Christ was the Son of God and when we reached the zoo I did. Birds and blue bells and wallabies hopping all around." He was, from that point on, a new man.

Introduction to *The Great Divorce*

Before exploring *The Great Divorce,* I want to make some comments about its basic theme and structure. Lewis actually began developing the idea for the book back in 1931 when as a new Christian, he came across the writings of Jeremy Taylor, a seventeenth-century Anglican divine, and Prudentius, a fourth-century poet and hymn writer. Inspired by those writings, Lewis began gathering ideas for a book that would follow a group of damned souls on holiday from hell to heaven. Lewis began work on his novel many years later, and it was finally published in 1945.

The novel begins with a preface that alludes to William Blake's poem *The Marriage of Heaven and Hell,* where Lewis states,

> Blake wrote the Marriage of Heaven and Hell. If I have written of their Divorce, this is not because I think myself a fit antagonist for so great a genius, nor even because I feel at all sure that I know what he meant. But in some sense or other, the attempt to make that marriage is perennial. The attempt is based on the belief that reality never presents us with an absolutely unavoidable "either-or" . . . that mere development or adjustment or refinement will somehow turn evil into good. . . . This belief I take to be a disastrous error. . . . Evil can be undone, but it cannot "develop" into good.

The novel that then transpires is predicated on this belief that no marriage or joining of heaven and hell, good and evil, the redeemed and the unredeemed is possible in eternity. Lewis urges his readers to remember that his novel is fantasy, not an attempt at systematic theology.

Lewis's title is packed with theological and symbolic meaning. In contrast to Blake's "marriage" of heaven and hell, he writes of their permanent divorce. God uses the metaphor of marriage throughout Scripture to help us understand the incredible benefits of salvation and relationship with himself. In the Old Testament, God repeatedly accuses the Israelites of spiritual adultery when they reject him in favor of other gods, kings, materialism, and so on.

The Book of Hosea particularly illustrates this marriage and adultery concept.

In the New Testament, Christ is symbolized as a bridegroom, and the church (all Christians) is the bride. We are commanded to wait expectantly for our returning groom. The Book of Revelation develops this marriage image vividly in the contrast between the harlot of Babylon in Revelation 17 and the amazing marriage imagery of Christ and his bride, the church, in Revelation 19.

Relying on all this biblical imagery, Lewis creates a title that helps the reader understand the magnitude of our rejection of God. In the same way that marriage is the apex of human relationship, security, and intimacy, so is divorce the devastation of all those ideals and dreams. Lewis uses the definite article *the* as a reminder that there is only one spiritual divorce—the central divorce of all existence—humanity's rejection of God. The juxtaposition of *great* and *divorce* becomes an oxymoron, for no one would describe even an amicable divorce as great, in the standard connotation of the word. Lewis is clearly using *great* in another way. His *great* is a word of magnitude, significance, and irony. Furthermore, our divorce from God is not *a* divorce but rather *the* divorce. Human divorce and its pain are but a mere shadow of the schism between God and us when we reject grace.

Finally, *divorce* implies pain, rejection, lost hopes and dreams, fracture, infidelity, insecurity, impermanency, and much more. Marriage, by God's standard, is intended to be eternal; divorce legally ends what was (and is) eternal. Just as in marriage two become one, so humanity was created to be in relationship with the Creator. When that intended relationship remains broken, we feel the brokenness and anger of the divorce. Because marriage offers the most intimate of human relationships, the tragic loss of that intimacy is the closest analogy to the eternal loss of relationship with God.

Having established a biblical context with his title, Lewis gradually reveals his novel's genre: fantasy. This becomes apparent in the first chapter, although not immediately. The book's first-person narrator introduces us to the setting by telling us about a dreary, gray, and drizzly town trapped in a perpetual twilight. Although he has walked for hours, he has seen no one, and even the shops seem deserted. Therefore, when he notices people lining up at a public bus stop, he joins the group with relief. Yet he immediately notices they are a miserable bunch—quarreling, pushing, and swindling each other at every opportunity. By the time the anticipated bus arrives, only a few people remain in the line, for the others have gone home angry. The narrator boards the bus rather hesitantly, and at that point, Lewis begins to introduce his characters, setting, and literary mode.

As the narrator interacts with his fellow passengers, he learns more about the gray town that they all just left. He is told that everyone quarrels continuously, and so people move farther and farther from each other. That is why the town seems deserted; its residents are incapable of relationship and therefore move farther and farther from each other. The narrator also learns that the houses, shops, and commodities of the gray town are merely imaginary and therefore cannot offer any gratification or satisfaction. People can imagine a house, for instance, but the imaginary house cannot keep out the rain, wind, or other threats. They can likewise imagine food, but it offers no fulfillment.

One of the passengers reveals that there is a rumor that the perpetual state of twilight will soon come to an end and be replaced by permanent night and absolute darkness. At that point, another passenger, an Anglican bishop, interjects his opinion. "No," he says, "that is nonsense and there is not a shred of evidence that this twilight is going to turn into a night. There has been a revolution of opinion on that in educated circles and I am surprised you haven't heard of it. All the nightmare fantasies of our ancestors have been swept away and what we see now in this subdued and delicate half-light is the promise of a dawn." Doesn't that sound familiar? With this character, Lewis alludes to the popular optimism that so characterizes liberal churchmen.

It is important to notice that Lewis's hell deliberately contrasts wih the traditional view of hell as a place of physical torment, fire, brimstone, thirst, and so on. Instead, his hell is depicted as a distorted little town. Furthermore, it soon becomes apparent that the gray town is the antithesis of Lewis's heaven. It is dark, dead, lonely, and dissatisfying—something of a cosmic morgue.

From the outset Lewis's characters are interesting but unappealing. Some are belligerent while others are whiny and insipid. This, too, is significant. Popular conceptions of hell tend to assume that character will be unaffected by damnation, but Lewis suggests quite the opposite. His novel implies that the blessing of common grace present in this world will be completely absent in hell. Here in time, even in the context of an imperfect, fallen world, love, friendship, honor, and selflessness are still possible, despite their distorted manifestations. That is because God is present in his world, and with his presence, his attributes. That will not be true of hell, however. Hell is the one place in the universe where God denies his presence. Therefore, hell will be the absence of God's three primary attributes as revealed in Scripture: life, light, and love. That is why Lewis depicts it as a morgue-like place. If God is the source of those goods, then hell must be characterized by their opposites: death, darkness, and hate. Lewis's characters then illustrate that absence of love in their inability to relate on any meaningful level with each other. Hell then becomes a place of absolute alienation, with its inhabitants living millions of miles apart from one another—by choice. This again suggests the divorce concept of the title.

The bus ride becomes Lewis's medium by which he cues the reader that this is a fantasy novel, for suddenly the bus begins to fly. A short time later, a gun and knife battle breaks out among the passengers, but no one is injured. It is then that the reader begins to understand that these characters are already dead. Soon, light envelopes the bus, and the characters view a looming cliff as the bus flies nearly vertically toward heaven. This is the point at which the story becomes particularly fascinating.

The ghosts' arrival in heaven feels somewhat anticlimactic, for none of them seem pleased to be there. Some are afraid to leave the bus, while others begin to explore suspiciously. No one enjoys or appreciates heaven's beauty. Again, Lewis reminds the reader of the soul condition of the damned. In rejecting God they have rejected joy. They are incapable, apart from salvation and regeneration, from participating in the joys of heaven despite its evident superiority to hell.

The narrator notes that when he arrives in heaven, he feels "the sense of being in a larger space, perhaps even a larger *sort* of space, than [he] had ever known before: as if the sky were further off and the extent of the green plain wider than they could be on . . . earth. [He] had got 'out' in some sense which made the Solar System itself seem an indoor affair." That is a delightful image of heaven!

It is then, though, that the narrator realizes, to his horror, that he and his fellow passengers are all ghosts. He had not noticed this before, but now in the light and solidity of heaven, their insubstantiality becomes obvious. Lewis describes his ghosts as "man-shaped stains on the brightness of that air." The ghosts are so insubstantial that they are unable to make any impact on heaven. Their feet do not bend the grass or disturb the dewdrops. In fact, the blades of grass pierce through their ghostly feet. The vastness of heaven leaves the ghosts feeling ironically exposed and vulnerable, naked and terribly insubstantial. It is not that they have changed, however. They have merely been revealed for what they have always been. This is confirmed by the narrator, who states, "The men were as they always had been; as all the men I had known had been perhaps. It was the light, the grass, the trees that were different."

What we see next are a series of characters who illustrate the excuses (or the "grounds for divorce") of those people who reject God. Lewis uses episodes or vignettes to illustrate these divorces. Each gray-town resident is met by a heavenly resident, someone he or she had known in life, who tries to persuade the ghost to begin the journey toward the mountains and "Deep Heaven." The bright, heavenly people explain that heaven will hurt at first, but with each step, it will hurt a little less. This is a portrait of the idea that redemption is progressive—a movement away from pride and arrogance and the false claim that having our own way is better than having God's way.

Every one of these characters has a fixed idea of the way things ought to be, and each tries to blackmail God by asserting that he doesn't cooperate with their preconceived notions of what heaven should be; thus they want nothing of God or heaven.

Episode 1: The Big Ghost

The first episode of the novel involves a man who insists on "having his rights." This fellow is shocked when his heavenly guide turns out to be a coworker who murdered one of their mutual friends. Stunned, he declares, "Personally, . . . I'd have thought you and I ought to be the other way round." He then goes on to assert, "I've been straight all my life. I don't say I was a religious man and I don't say I didn't have my faults. Far from it. But I did my best by everybody all my life, see? That's the sort of chap I was. I never had anything that wasn't mine by rights."

This Big Ghost demands his rights: "I'm just asking for nothing but my rights. You may think you can put me down because you dress up like that but you weren't when you worked under me. Well, I'm only a poor man. I've got my rights, same as you, see?" At this, the spirit of the man who worked for him replies, "Oh, it's not as bad as that. I haven't got my rights, or I should not be here. You will not get yours either. You will get something far better."

Lewis makes a vitally important point here. The human perception of morality and justice is horribly skewed. When we naively demand our rights or justice, we are demanding God's judgment. The Bible declares, "For the wages of sin is death, but the free gift of God is eternal life in Christ Jesus our Lord." The Big Ghost fails to grasp this, for he retorts, "I'm not asking for anybody's bleeding charity." His former friend then interjects, "Then do. At once. Ask for the Bleeding Charity. Everything is here for the asking and nothing can be bought." Unconvinced, the man says, "I done my best." To this assertion his friend says, "You can never do it like that. Your feet will never grow hard enough to walk on our grass that way, if you try it on your own works. You will get tired before you get to the mountains. And, by the way it isn't exactly true. . . . You weren't a decent man and you didn't do your best. None of us were and none of us did but it doesn't matter, there is no need to go into that now."

Most people entertain inflated views of themselves, and their sense of self-sufficiency is actually the very thing that keeps them from God. Despite the best efforts of his friend to invite him into joy, the Big Ghost ultimately exclaims, "Tell them I'm not coming. I'd rather be damned than go along with you. I've got my rights, see. I don't need to go sniveling along tied to your apron strings." So, he returns to the bus and ultimately hell. He offers an example of those who confuse morality for holiness.

Episode 2: The Bishop

Next, the narrator observes an encounter between a spirit and an Anglican bishop. This bishop represents those who deny intellectual sins. He argues that his sincerity cannot be condemned, saying, "My views were honest and heroic. I asserted them fearlessly. When the doctrine of the resurrection ceased to commend itself to the critical faculties that God had given me, I openly rejected it. I preached my famous sermon, I defied the whole chapter, and I took every risk." His guide then responds, "What risk? What was it all likely to come to except more popularity and more sales for your books?" The bishop says, "This is unkind of you. What are you suggesting?" The spirit answers, "Do you really think there are no sins of intellect?" Finally, their encounter comes down to a final demand by the bishop before he will agree to the journey: "I should want a guarantee that you are taking me to a place where I shall find a wider sphere of usefulness." To this the spirit replies, "No, I can promise none of these things. No sphere of usefulness: you are not needed there at all. No scope for your talents: only forgiveness for having perverted them. No atmosphere for inquiry, for I will bring you to the land not of questions but of answers, and you shall see the face of God."

Yet the fellow ultimately refuses to accompany his former friend. The offer is actually an offense to his taste. In a final plea, his guide says, "Listen! Once you were a child. Once you knew what inquiry was for. There was a time when you asked questions because you wanted answers. . . . You have gone far wrong. Thirst was made for water; inquiry for truth." But the bishop's ghost refuses the offer. He argues that *for him,* "God is . . . the spirit of sweetness and light and tolerance . . . and service." Furthermore, he remembers that he had promised to give a lecture down in the gray town, discussing if Jesus had lived longer, what his more mature views might have been. He laments Jesus' premature death and his promising life that was cut so short.

In other words, the bishop rejects the real God in favor of one of his own making. He denies the possibility of sins of the intellect, denies the deity of Christ, chooses futile inquiry over truth, and commits himself to misery instead of embracing joy.

Episode 3: Ikey

As he continues on, the narrator observes a ghost peering suspiciously around him. He recalls the Big Ghost calling this ghost Ikey, and he begins to watch the creature. The ghost is bent on picking up some apples lying nearby, but eventually he abandons his attempt to pick up *apples* and resorts to "trying to find if there was *one* small enough to carry." For the apples, like everything else in heaven, are more solid and real than the ghost and feel as heavy as lead. He finally finds one small enough to carry, and he sets out on his "*via dolorosa*," carrying his heavenly commodity. Suddenly a voice booms, "Fool. Put it down. . . . You cannot take it back. There is not room for it in Hell. Stay here and learn to eat such apples." Ironically, the ghost has no intention of trying to enjoy the apple; his goal is to sell it, and his sin is avarice—materialism. He ultimately rejects God's offer of true enjoyment in favor of his greed.

Episode 4: The Cynical Ghost

After his encounter with Ikey, the narrator meets a cynical and rather "hard-bitten" ghost. His grounds for divorce from God are related to his selfishness and mistrust. He views heaven merely as some unearthly tourist trap, asserting that it (like the sites on earth, and even hell itself) is run by management that is always bent on taking advantage of everyone. When the narrator suggests that heaven is supposedly run by different management, the ghost cynically denies that possibility. He then reveals the heart of his complaint when he says, "It's up to the Management to find something that doesn't bore us, isn't it? It's their job." Like so many people, this ghost misunderstands heaven. He has come to believe in heaven merely as a gimmick, a distraction from boredom, and something designed to suit his personal whims.

What he fails to recognize, however, is that he doesn't even know what his needs and desires are. He is incapable of envisioning a satisfactory heaven, not because he wants something more spectacular but because his desires are far too small. People often think of heaven in terms of a place that will perpetually amuse them—a personal utopia—but such a view reduces heaven tragically. Heaven is where we know and enjoy God himself. Every distraction that we pursue throughout life merely reflects the true longing, whether we realize it or not. What the cynical ghost fails to acknowledge is his own inadequacy. He refuses the "solidification" process whereby he would be able to enjoy God and heaven.

Episode 5: The Self-Conscious Ghost

The narrator next observes a female ghost attempting unsuccessfully to hide behind some bushes. She is horrified by her transparency and feels exposed and vulnerable. Throughout her life she hid behind her external image, but in heaven this is no longer possible; there, people are revealed. Her heavenly guide assures her that her shame will pass quickly if she will just go with her toward the mountains. Yet the self-conscious ghost exclaims, "But I would rather die." Her guide then responds, "You have died already. There is no good trying to go back to that." When this pathetic little ghost asks why she was even born, her guide answers that she was born for "infinite happiness. Step out into it at any moment."

The spirit then explains the nature of shame and obsessive introspection in this way: "Don't you remember that there were things too hot to touch with your finger but you could drink them all right? Shame is like that if you accept it and drink the cup to the bottom and find it very nourishing." Again, the idea of swallowing one's pride becomes the key. The spirit guide then pleads with the ghost, saying, "Friend, could you, only for a moment, fix your mind on something not yourself?" This question encapsulates the awful effects of the fall and the sin nature; we were made for God, but sin has resulted in a psychopathic preoccupation with self that precludes our ability to see and enjoy God. There is an uncertain outcome at the end of this encounter, for we are not told whether the ghost retreats or moves closer toward "Deep Heaven."

Episode 6: George MacDonald

It is at this point in the novel that our narrator meets his own guide, George MacDonald. MacDonald was to C. S. Lewis what Virgil was to Dante—a literary model and mentor. This is why he appears now to guide the narrator. It is also MacDonald who clarifies the images of heaven and hell for the reader. He explains that the narrator is not truly in heaven yet, not "Deep Heaven." Rather, he is in what MacDonald calls the "Valley of the Shadow of Death." He then goes on to explain a little of the nature of sin and damnation: "[Those who reject God] say of some temporal suffering, no future bliss can make up for temporal suffering. Not knowing that heaven, once attained, works backwards and will turn even that agony into a glory. And of some sinful pleasure they say 'Let me but have *this* and I'll take the consequence.'" How many of us have found ourselves making that same gamble? We foolishly believe that the gratification of a desire could outweigh the glories of heaven and enjoyment of God.

MacDonald then continues by explaining that such people fail to understand

> how damnation will spread back and back into their past and contaminate the pleasure of the sin. Both processes begin before death. The good man's past begins to change and his forgiven sins and sorrows take on the quality of heaven. The bad man's past already conforms to his badness and is filled only with dreariness. That is why, at the end of all things, when the

> sun rises here and the twilight turns to blackness down there, the blessed will say we have never lived anywhere except in heaven and the lost always in hell and both will speak truly.

Here Lewis offers a profound hypothesis. He asserts that if we choose earthly goods above God and heaven, we miss out on the joys of both and actually transform earth into a hell. Yet if we choose God, we will one day discover that redemption worked backward, and even life's worst pains—life's worst moments—were, in fact, used redemptively by God to prepare the soul for heaven and joy. We will realize then that there was no evil that could destroy God's purposes or thwart his redemptive work.

As they walk along, the narrator and MacDonald encounter a grumbling ghost. This encounter prompts the narrator to ask why a seemingly minor sin such as grumbling should be punished by damnation. MacDonald answers, "The question is whether she is a grumbler, or only a grumble. If there is still a real woman—even the least trace of one—still there inside the grumbling, it can be brought to life again." This answer confuses the narrator, who then asks how there could be a grumble without a grumbler. MacDonald responds, "The whole difficulty of understanding Hell is that the thing to be understood is so nearly Nothing. . . . It begins with a grumbling mood, and yourself still distinct from it: perhaps criticizing it. . . . Ye can repent and come out of it again. But there may come a day when you can do that no longer. Then there will be no you left to criticize the mood, nor even to enjoy it, just the grumble itself going on forever like a machine." With this discussion, Lewis further explores the nature of sin and damnation. He asserts that eventually, we are absorbed into sin and essentially obscured by it.

Lewis clarified this concept in the second book of his space trilogy, *Perelandra,* when he wrote, "There was, no doubt, a confusion of persons in damnation: what Pantheists falsely hoped of Heaven bad men really received in Hell. They were melted down into their Master, as a lead soldier slips down and loses his shape in the ladle held over the gas ring. The question of whether Satan, or one whom Satan had digested, is acting on any given occasion, has in the long run no clear significance." In this episode of *The Great Divorce* and in *Perelandra*, Lewis asserts that damnation is the reduction of humanity into something that is nearly nothing. Contrary to our foolish and naive view of sin, it does not lead to power but rather to powerlessness.

MacDonald then explains to the narrator, "There are only two kinds of people in the end: those who say to God, 'Thy will be done,' and those to whom God says, in the end, '*Thy* will be done.' All that are in Hell, choose it. Without that self-choice there could be no Hell. No soul that seriously and constantly desires joy will ever miss it. Those who seek find. To those who knock it is opened."

Episode 7: The Flirtatious Ghost

As MacDonald and the narrator move away from the grumbling ghost, a pitiful female ghost draws their attention. The narrator comments, "Her problem was quite the opposite of that which afflicted the [self-conscious ghost]. This one seemed quite unaware of her phantasmal appearance. . . . She supposed herself still capable of attracting [men] and was trying to do so. . . . If a corpse already liquid with decay had arisen from the coffin, smeared its gums with lipstick, and attempted a flirtation, the result could not have been more appalling." With this short episode, Lewis conveys again the tragic nature of self and sin. This poor ghost sees herself only as an objectification of lust. She is unaware of the value of her own soul, and therefore she has forfeited true love for something temporal and illusionary; she has mistaken sexual attraction for genuine love.

Episode 8: The Artist

One of the most interesting encounters in the novel is between a heavenly guide and the ghost of an artist. As the ghost gazes about at the landscape of heaven, he exclaims, "God!" His spirit guide responds, "God what? . . . In our grammar *God* is a noun." Lewis creatively uses grammar to reveal the contrast between the two characters' views of God. For the artist ghost, "god" is reduced to merely an explicative; for the guide, God is magnified as the source of all that is good. The artist ghost, however, shows no interest in God; he has only taken the offer of the heaven tour because he wants to paint it.

His guide then explains that is something he can't yet do: "When you painted on earth . . . it was because you caught glimpses of Heaven in the landscape. The success of your painting was that it enabled others to see the glimpses too. But here you are having the thing itself. It is from here the messages came. There is no good *telling* us about this country, for we see it already. In fact we see it better than you do." This artist has become so focused on his art that it has become merely an extension of his ego. His spirit guide points this out, saying, "Every poet and musician and artist, but for Grace, is drawn away from love of the thing he tells, to love of the telling, till, down in Deep Hell, they cannot be interested in God at all but only in what they say about Him."

Again, Lewis uses this scene to emphasize an important point. Every earthly gift, properly received, is meant to reveal God. Every attempt to enjoy the temporal gifts, including talents, apart from God becomes self-destructive and futile. Essentially he illustrates the plight Solomon conveys in Ecclesiastes when he asks rhetorically, "For who can eat and who can have enjoyment without Him?" (Ecclesiastes 2:25). The answer is no one. Unfortunately, this ghost fails to grasp that truth, and he abandons God and heaven in favor of hell.

Episode 9: The Manipulative Wife

This is perhaps one of the more darkly amusing heavenly encounters. This ghost was once a wife, and she exercised her lust for power by controlling every moment of her poor husband's life. Her exalted view of herself led her to a reduced view of his value until he eventually became nothing more than a means by which she could feel powerful. Ironically, the poor husband has escaped her in death, for he is in heaven and she is in hell. Yet her desire is not to join her spouse in heaven but to drag him back to hell so that she can "have someone to—to do things to." She observes, "It's simply frightful down there. No one minds about me at all. I can't alter them." Near the end of the encounter with her guide, the angry wife says, "He is not fit to be on his own. Put me in charge of him. He wants firm handling. I know him better than you do. Please, I am so miserable." Here Lewis relates yet another ground for divine divorce. This pathetic wife would obtain power at any cost. In elevating her own will to the status of a god, she has lost all capacity to love or be loved. She admits her misery yet rejects the only solution to it.

Episode 10: Michael's Mother

This encounter exposes the danger of idolatry by introducing a ghost who has come on the guided tour of heaven only in order to find her son and take him back with her to hell. She views God and heaven only as a means to reunite with her son. She is met by her brother, who, like her son, is a resident of heaven. When she declares her willingness to "do whatever's necessary" to see her son, her guide interjects, "You're treating God only as a means to Michael." He then explains the "thickening" process is dependent on her "learning to want God for His own sake." He explains that "you cannot love a fellow-creature fully till you love God." Yet Pam, the mother, refuses to accept this. She eventually retorts in anger, "I hate your religion, and I hate and despise your God." In a childish fit of rage, she screams, "No one has a right to come between me and my son. Not even God. Tell Him that to His face. I want my boy, and I mean to have him. He is mine, do you understand? Mine, mine, mine, for ever and ever."

As the narrator and MacDonald walk away from this miserable scene, MacDonald explains its meaning, saying, "Brass is mistaken for gold more easily than clay is." With this statement, he identifies the mother's grounds for divorcing God; she loves only herself and rejects all other loves. What she asserts as love for Michael is only a twisted self-absorption, for she would remove him from heaven and take him with her to hell merely for her own gratification. Her love has become a false god, and therefore her natural affection has become first distorted and finally destroyed.

A. W. Tozer dealt with this same theme in his interpretation of the biblical account of Abraham's obedience to God when God told him to sacrifice Isaac. Isaac was the beloved son of promise, the delight of the old man's life. And yet, when Abraham chose God over Isaac, he learned an invaluable lesson. Tozer says through this circumstance, the potential loss of Abraham's son, God was, in effect, saying, "It's all right, Abraham. I never intended that you should actually slay the lad. I only wanted to remove him from the temple of your heart that I might reign unchallenged there. I wanted to correct the perversion that existed in your love. Now you may have the boy, sound and well. Take him and go back to your tent." (Tozer, *The Pursuit of God*, chap. 2).

Here is the key point: when Abraham gave his love wholeheartedly to God, even over his love for his child, he did not lose what he loved—he gained it! Had he chosen Isaac, Isaac would likely have become an idol, eventually rendering Abraham incapable of love. But when Abraham chose God, he received, as the adage goes, God and everything besides. This is what those who reject God so fail to grasp. The proposition is not "God-or"; it is "God-and."

Episode 11: The Man with the Lizard

Along the lines of the misconception we just discussed, many people mistakenly believe that following God requires an ascetic self-denial. While Jesus commanded that we are to deny ourselves, take up the cross, and follow him, that does not mean the Christian life is one of meaningless self-denial. Quite the opposite, in fact. In John 10:10 Jesus declares, "I came that they may have life, and have it abundantly." Yet somehow we are suspicious of God's motives, fearing that he does not really know what we need. This is the sin of this next ghost.

As the narrator and MacDonald continue on, they encounter a young man with a small red lizard on his shoulder. The lizard is whispering something in the man's ear, and the man responds to the whispers by telling the lizard to "shut up." Just then, a glowing angel confronts the man, asking a simple question: "Would you like me to make him quiet?" When the man says he would, the angel answers, "Then I will kill him." The man then recoils in horror, for he had not anticipated such drastic action. He responds, "Thanks for your hospitality. But it's no good, you see. I told this little chap," speaking of the lizard, "that he would have to be quiet if he came—which he insisted on doing. Of course his stuff won't do here: I realize that. But he won't stop. I shall just have to go home."

Insistent, the angel continues, "It's the only way. . . . Shall I kill it?" The man again responds, "Well, that is a further question. I am quite open to consider it but it is important issue, isn't it. For the moment, I was only thinking about silencing it because it is so damned embarrassing. . . . There is time to discuss that later. . . . No, no, don't bother. Sorry to be such a nuisance. Look, it has gone to sleep on its own accord. I am sure it will be all right. Thank you, so much."

Yet the angel persists in repeating, "May I kill it?" Notice that he poses the offer as a question because the angel cannot act contrary to the man's choice; that freedom cannot be violated. The angel explains this when he says, "I cannot kill it against your will. It is impossible. Have I your permission?" It is then that the lizard speaks audibly for the first time, saying to the man, "Be careful. He can do what he says. He can kill me. One fatal word from you and he *will*! Then you'll be without me for ever and ever. It's not natural. How could you live? You'd be only a sort of ghost, not a real man as you are now. He doesn't understand. He's only a cold, bloodless abstract thing. . . . I admit I've sometimes gone too far in the past, but I promise I won't do it again. I'll give you nothing but really nice dreams—all sweet and fresh and almost innocent."

Finally, the desperate man, still fearful of the possibility of either dying or of living without the lust on which he has grown dependent, yields and cries, "Do what you like, God help me, God help me." The scene that transpires is perhaps one of the most inspiring in literature, for as the angel kills the lizard and flings it to the ground, a transformation occurs:

> I saw . . . unmistakably solid but growing every moment solider, the upper arm and the shoulder of a man. Then, brighter still and stronger, the legs and hands. . . and if my attention had not wavered I should have seen the actual completing of a man. . . . What distracted me was the fact that at the same time something seemed to be happening to the lizard. . . . The creature was still struggling and even growing bigger. . . . Suddenly I started back, rubbing my eyes. What stood before me was the greatest stallion I have ever seen. . . . The new-made man turned and clapped the new horse's neck. . . . The man . . . flung himself at the feet of the Burning One, and embraced them. . . . In joyous haste the young man leaped upon the horse's back. Turning in his seat he waved a farewell. . . . I saw them winding up, scaling what seemed impossible steeps . . . till . . . they vanished.

Then, as the narrator gazes in wonder, he hears nature itself begin to sing: "*The Master says to our master, Come up. Share my rest and splendour till all natures that were your enemies become slaves to dance before you and backs for you to ride, and firmness for your feet to rest on.*"

The meaning of this episode is profound. To allude again to Christ's promise of abundant life, what God offers is not reductionistic but expansive. He promises to take those weak, controlling desires that we cling to and to exchange them for true joy. Those aspects of our natures that were our enemies will—in him—become "slaves to dance before us" and "firmness for [our] feet to rest on." And, lest we make the mistake of thinking that sin can be transformed into goodness, the angel explains, "Nothing, not even the best and noblest, can go on as it is now. Nothing, not even what is lowest and most bestial, will not be raised again if it submits to death. It is sown a natural body, it is raised a spiritual body." This is Lewis's rendition of the death of the old nature. It is killed, and then God replaces it with a new one, empowered in and through Christ and the Holy Spirit's regenerative work.

Episode 12: The Tragedian

Near the end of the novel, the narrator observes a strange encounter. He sees a tall, dramatic-looking man, accompanied by a very small man who reminds him of an organ-grinder's monkey. The two are connected by a chain, but only the tall man speaks. The pair are met by a beautiful woman followed by an entourage of spirits, animals, children, and light. The woman walks right up to the strange duo and begins to speak to the little man, asking his forgiveness. Ironically, it is the tragedian who answers condescendingly. When the woman invites the man (whom we learn was her husband in life) into Love, the tragedian responds, "Love! . . . Do you know the meaning of the word?" The woman then explains, "What we called love down there was mostly the craving to be loved. In the main I loved you for my own sake: because I needed you." She then explains that in heaven, she has no needs: "I am full now, not empty. I am in Love Himself, not lonely. Strong, not weak. You shall be the same. Come and see. We shall have no *need* for one another now: we can begin to love truly." "She needs me no more, no more," the tragedian responds.

Meanwhile, the little man on the end of a chain becomes smaller and smaller as he lets his false self dominate. As a last resort, through the vehicle of the tragedian, the husband attempts a sort of emotional blackmail, accusing his wife of not loving him in the hope that she pity him and give in to his demands. As to this matter of blackmail, MacDonald explains, "Either the day must come when joy prevails and all the makers of misery are no longer able to infect it; or else for ever and ever the makers of misery can destroy in others the happiness they reject for themselves. I know it has a grand sound to say ye'll accept no salvation which leaves one creature in the dark outside. But, watch that sophistry or you will make a Dog in a Manger the tyrant of the universe."This, by the way, was an expression for a person who resented anyone else enjoying what he himself could not enjoy.

MacDonald explains that such blackmail is what "draws men to concede what should not be conceded and to flatter when they should speak the truth. . . . It was used as a weapon by bad men against good ones." He then adds, "Every disease that submits to a cure shall be cured: but we will not call blue yellow to please those who insist on still having jaundice, nor make a midden of the world's garden for the sake of some who cannot abide the smell of roses."

This encounter then leads into a discussion of the nature of hell itself, for the narrator asks why the wife did not descend to hell to get her husband. MacDonald answers by getting down on his knees and pointing to a crack in the ground with a blade of grass. He says that he cannot be sure through which crack the bus ascended, but it came up through a crack no bigger than the one to which he points. The narrator is perplexed, so MacDonald continues,

> All hell is smaller than one pebble of your earthly world: but it is smaller than one atom of *this* world, the Real World. Look at yon butterfly. If it swallowed all Hell, Hell would not be big enough to do it any harm or to have any taste. . . . For a damned soul is nearly nothing: it is shrunk, shut up in itself. Good beats upon the damned incessantly as sound waves beat on the ears of the deaf, but they cannot receive it. Their fists are clenched, their teeth are clenched, their eyes fast shut. First they will not, in the end they cannot, open their hands for gifts, or their mouths for food, or their eyes to see.

Through MacDonald, Lewis then explains that only God could make himself small enough to descend to the level of the damned and save them.

Final Episode

At the end of the story, Lewis introduces a very complex image, the image of a chess game. His narrator observes a large chessboard, on which small figures move "to and fro." Around the chessboard stand men and women, each of whom is represented by an *idolum* on the board. The narrator asks in horror, "Then is all that I have been seeing in this country false? These conversations . . . were they only the mimicry of choices that had really been made ages ago?" To this, MacDonald answers, "Or might ye not as well say, anticipations of a choice to be made at the end of all things? But ye'd do better to say neither. Ye saw the choices a bit more clearly than ye could see them on earth: the lens was clearer." With this statement, Lewis encapsulates the goal of this novel. Through it, he is trying to help his reader, like his fictional narrator, grasp his choice more clearly. Life and time offer two options: marriage or divorce. Both are eternal in nature. And in life as in chess, our choices can checkmate us while we remain unaware of our doom. For instance, it is possible to lose a chess match many moves before the actual checkmate concludes the game and yet to play on, oblivious to the fatal error.

Similarly, all our choices in time reflect either a desire to know and follow God or a desire to gratify our own wills. It has been said that if we do not choose God, it matters not what else we choose. This was illustrated in a conversation between Christ and Peter in John 6, when many followers were abandoning Jesus, and he turns to his disciples and says, "You do not want to go away also, do you?" Peter then responds with what should be the response of all of us: "Lord, to whom shall we go? You have words of eternal life. We have believed and have come to know that You are the Holy One of God" (vv. 67–69).

Life is not merely a game of strategy—it is the temporal opportunity to grasp that Jesus Christ is the only source of life. Any step (or move) we take away from Jesus Christ is a step toward potential damnation and misery.

It is at this point in the novel, then, that Lewis's narrator suddenly finds himself enveloped in light. Fearing that time has come to an end, and the eternal day and night have replaced choice, he screams, "The morning! The morning! I am caught by the morning and I am a ghost!" Yet this is not the case. The narrator awakes from what has been a dream. He has been awakened by air raid sirens and in his fright has pulled the tablecloth from his study table, pummeling himself with falling books. Like Dante in the *Divine Comedy,* Lewis, the character, awakes to find his afterlife merely a dream; opportunity and redemption still remain available to him, yet his dream has increased his sense of urgency and helped him grasp the significance of his temporal choices.

Conclusion

The bottom line is that this marvelous story reminds us that life is essentially a soul-forming process. We are moving either toward God or away from him. The humility of moving toward God requires us to deny our own idea of where happiness lies and to begin to embrace God's desire for our lives. It involves the realization that we do not know what our best interest looks like, but he does. It is the realization that God actually does want the best for us and that he alone can make it happen. It is the realization that we must humble ourselves under his mighty hand so that he can exalt us at the proper time, when all the pain and sorrow that we now experience will be as nothing in comparison to a moment of the pleasure of his presence.

Lewis draws some important principles through this genre of fiction. Essentially, he stresses three key points: (1) We cannot fix or establish a point beyond which a person is unable to repent, but there will be such a point somewhere. Lewis talks about a point of no return, where a choice is made to either accept God or reject him. This is a rather horrifying thought. (2) Even God will not overrule free will because it is meaningless to talk of people doing freely what they have freely made impossible for themselves. In *The Problem of Pain*, for example, Lewis deals with this whole issue of why God hasn't met everyone in heaven, and the question he raises is, "With, or against their will?" Suppose a man has been seeking to avoid God all his life? What makes us suppose he will suddenly enjoy God's presence? We are moving either toward God or away from him, and heaven or hell becomes the ultimate destiny entailed in that choice. (3) Lewis illustrates a concept connoted in the word *fissiparous*. The word *fission* is a part of *fissiparous*, and it implies the breaking up of something. Sin is fissiparous and can never, in a thousand eternities, find a way to arrest its own reproduction. Hell, then, was created as a tourniquet to stop the lost soul's downward progression. To put it another way, Lewis says that "the ripening of good and evil has a way of moving us toward one or the other and that good continues to ripen and that evil continues to ripen as well."

He also asserts, "Evil can be undone but it cannot be developed into good. Time does not heal it. The spell must be unwound bit by bit; with backward mutters of disappearing power or else not." He goes on, "If we insist on keeping hell, or even earth, we shall not see heaven. If we select heaven, we shall not be able to retain even the smallest and intimate souvenirs of hell." Redemption is an all-or-nothing process.

Finally, Lewis assures us that if we choose God, we will not be disappointed: "I believe, to be sure, that any man who reaches heaven will find that what he abandoned, even if he plucked out his right eye, was precisely nothing, that the kernel of what he was seeking, even in his most depraved wishes, will be there, beyond his expectation, waiting for him in the high countries."

God has given us the immense dignity of choice. We are called to choose the way we are to go. We are given the choice that Joshua so eloquently articulated in Joshua 24:15 when he said to the Israelites, "Choose for yourselves today whom you will serve: whether the gods which your fathers served which were beyond the River, or the gods of the Amorites in whose land you are living; but as for me and my house, we will serve the LORD." As Lewis illustrates so poignantly in this novel, life is a serious, wonderful thing. God has offered us infinite love; he has extended an offer of eternal union. The response is ours. Eternal *marriage* or eternal divorce—this is the choice of life.

Lord, we thank you for this time together, and I ask that we would understand more about the glories that you have prepared for us, glories that we can scarcely begin to grasp. As your Word says, you have told us of things we cannot understand, "things which eye has not seen and ear has not heard, and which have not entered the heart of man, all that God has prepared for those who love Him." Let us be the people who pursue the good that you desire for us. May we seek the joy that cannot be separated from you but can only be found in you. We pray in Jesus' name. Amen.

NOTES

NOTES

FRANÇOIS FÉNELON

Christian Perfection

Introduction

The works of François Fénelon had a profound and controversial impact on his own time and own generation. A Catholic scholar and theologian, he became instrumental in a movement that swept through France during the seventeenth century. This movement, termed quietism, suggested that the highest possible spiritual state necessitated a sort of self-annihilation, followed by an incorporation or absorption into the Divine—God. It generated controversy not merely because of its theological tenets but also because it emphasized the autonomy of its adherents and minimized church authority.

The Catholic Church ultimately condemned the movement and labeled its teachings heresy. The church asserted that quietism suggested a spiritual perfectibility during the temporal life that was not biblical. Furthermore, it contradicted Trinitarian theology, espoused pantheistic concepts of the nature of the soul, and asserted that an almost Buddhist-type meditative state led to the quietude of the mind and the perfection of the soul. Its most radical adherents even argued that the sacraments and law were eventually no longer applicable once a person had reached this inner, contemplative perfection.

Fénelon wrote and taught what has been termed "semi-quietism," a modified and less radical version of the original movement. Yet he, along with his friend Madame Guyon, stirred up significant theological controversy by promoting their unorthodox views. Fénelon's theological position eventually cost him much personally. He was a man who grew to understand suffering, for he experienced a tremendous amount of loss and pain in his life, partly as a result of choices that he himself made.

Fénelon was born in 1651 and died in 1715, but in his sixty-three years, he experienced an extraordinary wealth of opportunity. As a young man, he seemed headed toward tremendous prestige, wealth, and influence; but later in life he lost his job, his fame, his money, and many of his friends. Those losses were due, in part, to a deliberate choice he made because of his integrity; nevertheless, they caused him to understand the crucible of suffering. His teachings were forged in that crucible of affliction and adversity.

In many respects, Fénelon really was a man of sorrows and acquainted with grief. As a follower of Christ, he was profoundly influenced by the love of God and came to understand that to know God's love is the longing and quest of the human heart and the only means by which the heart will find rest.

There is definitely a mystical strain in Fénelon, and we will talk about that, yet it is counterbalanced by his very clear and keen mind. While he does teach a very real form of abandonment to divine providence, it is not characterized by a reckless passivity but rather by a proper submission to God's loving overtures and initiative in one's life.

Fénelon was born during France's golden age. Certainly this was a time, following the religious wars of the sixteenth century and the Thirty Years' War, when there was tremendous disillusionment with religious institutions. In part as a reaction to the religious fanaticism that some people encountered during these centuries, and the corruption and ineptitude of the church in some regards, there was a great flowering of art, music, literature, and philosophy. Alongside that artistic resurgence, however, was also a growing movement toward scientific rationalism. The new rationalism tended to discount revealed authority and church authority in favor of observation and experimentation. Its adherents emphasized the value of logic, scientific method, and deductive reasoning. Francis Bacon, for example, denounced the reliance on authority and Aristotelian logic, calling for a new scientific method of deductive generalization based on careful observation and experimentation. Then there was Galileo, with his science of mechanics and the application of the principles of geometry. Thomas Hobbes asserted that the principle of mechanics applied to every field of knowledge, and he argued the law of self-preservation as the basis for human behavior. René Descartes was so insistent on scientific rigor before accepting any belief that he denied even his own existence until he could prove it to be necessarily true. He argued mathematics as a model for all science.

There was a permeation of this kind of thinking on every level of French society, including the church, and it led to a movement away from the revealed truth and its impact on the heart. Because of this surge in rationalism, the idea of mysticism, especially of the medieval sort of Bernard of Clairvaux, William of St. Thierry, and others was regarded as something of an anachronism of the period, something that was really no longer relevant. So in that regard, Fénelon was a real oddity for his time in many ways.

It is necessary to establish a brief background and context for Fénelon's writings. He was a man whose spiritual correspondence has never been exceeded, and his letters exerted a remarkable influence. He corresponded with dignitaries and people at the French court, as well as simple people who lived in poverty. His writing dealt with a wide array of issues and topics.

There is a kind of spiritual direction and mentoring that takes place in Fénelon's letters, and they have been compiled into a number of books because they are full of remarkable counsel and advice. The one I will be focusing on is called *Christian Perfection*, and it was published several years ago by Bethany House. It is, unfortunately, now out of print. A few collections remain in print, however, and among them are *Meditations on the Heart of God*, *Talking with God*, and *The Seeking Heart*.

It is unfortunate that many people in the modern Christian

community have acquired an attraction to fluff and feel-good literature, simplistic works that contain very little substance. The vast bulk of such material will not even be around ten years from now, let alone in a hundred. That is just the nature of it. So, it is prudent to return to those classics that really nourish the soul, even though they sometimes seem remote to us. The old works often offer the very stuff that we need to be less parochial, less vulnerable to the prejudices and limitations of our own time. Frankly, despite the distance of several centuries, most people find that Fénelon is very accessible. His letters, generally speaking, are relevant and beneficial.

During the years that Fénelon was growing up, young Louis XIV firmly suppressed many disaffected nobles. He cleverly kept even the most powerful of them under his thumb by building the lavish palace of Versailles and holding endless balls and theatrical and musical performances to keep them happy; entertainment and complacency were the means by which he controlled the elite.

After his queen died in 1683, Louis married a devout Catholic named Madame de Maintenon, and she evidently exercised much influence over him, for it was around that time that he revoked the Edict of Nantes. This edict had been established almost a century before, in 1598. It had granted a measure of religious liberty to French Protestants, who had long endured significant persecution at the hands of the French Catholics. Louis's revocation of that liberty in 1685 created tremendous upheaval, resulting in the emigration of hundreds of thousands of French Protestants, called Huguenots, to other European countries and beyond. Ironically, the Huguenots were disproportionately influential in commerce and vital to the economic infrastructure of French society. Their mass migration out of France resulted in a significant loss in economic stability and was an incredible blunder from a historical standpoint. Fénelon's connection to this group was as a missionary of sorts. He and a number of other Catholic scholars/orators were sent to dissuade the Protestants from their beliefs and bring them into the fold of the Catholic Church.

Fénelon was raised in a noble family of significant financial means and political influence. He proved an adept scholar and was educated first by tutors and later at a series of elite and excellent schools. He was ordained as a priest into the Catholic Church in 1675 and served as a priest for the next decade or so. Then in 1686 the Bishop Bossuet commissioned him to serve in this capacity as a missionary to the Huguenots. Bossuet was one France's great orators; Fénelon was his oratorical match. It was largely due to his oratorical skills that Bossuet selected Fénelon. He sent him to work in an area that was the center of French Protestantism, and there his communication skills made him very effective. His gentle and gracious spirit actually won the hearts of some of the Protestants. He spent a year or two in that region.

He then returned to Paris, where he was elevated to the position of spiritual director to the Duke and Duchess of Beauvilliers and their family of eight daughters. At that time he wrote his first book, aptly on the education of little girls. It was a very perceptive work. The Duke of Beauvilliers was later named governor over the king's sons and grandsons, and because Fénelon was that family's spiritual counselor and rector, he exercised a profound though indirect impact on the French court through Beauvilliers.

Consequently, Fénelon was made personal tutor to the king's grandson, the young Duke of Burgundy. This was no trivial position, for the Duke of Burgundy was destined to become the next French king, Louis XV. It was Fénelon's mission, then, to prepare him for his future reign.

I must mention that this was not an easy task because it turns out that this young man proved to be an unholy terror from the very beginning. He was described in the following way: "He was immensely obstinate, desperately fond of hunting and good food, and of music and games which were dangerous to play. He could not endure to be beaten and he was disposed to be cruel and he looked upon the rest of mankind as an inferior race in which he had nothing in common. Even his brothers, who were supposed to be brought up the same as himself, were considered as just sort of a link between himself and the ordinary human race." This young fellow was the cause of much trouble. If when the clock struck the hour for dinner he wasn't ready to eat, he would simply break the clock. When he indulged in such fits of temper, people around him were told simply to be quiet and let them pass.

Yet Fénelon, after a few years, won the boy's heart, and over time, they developed a close relationship. The duke's whole personality altered in very remarkable ways because of Fénelon's influence. He matured into a young man of real virtue and devotion. Devout members of the court had great expectations because of Fénelon's influence on him, but unfortunately the Duke of Burgundy died before assuming the throne. The king's spoiled and completely inept great-grandson became the next French king. It is always interesting to speculate on what might have happened differently had he lived because even the slightest change would have had a reverberating historical impact. The point here, though, is that Fénelon exercised a tremendous influence in his time and was given positions of great privilege.

During the course of his life, Fénelon wrote several books, including *Fables*, which were moral lessons in the form of fairy tales, and *Dialogues of the Dead*, which sounds like a gruesome book but actually included bygone historical figures who told what they learned from life. This book is still reprinted from time to time. One of his more controversial books was a commentary on ethics titled *The Adventures of Telemachus*. It discussed how kings ought to reign and got Fénelon in much trouble later in his life when it became public; ironically, Fénelon had never intended it for publication.

In any case, as a result of serving as tutor to the heir of the French throne, he enjoyed access to the court of Versailles, where a number of devout Christians welcomed his presence. One of his correspondents was even the queen, Madame de Maintenon. Through evangelism and building relationally into their lives, he guided many spiritual children, and his friendship and correspondence with them continued throughout the rest of his life. We are the heirs to that correspondence.

Fénelon's early adult life was obviously characterized by numerous successes. He influenced people of significance and was regarded highly by church and secular officials. He was elevated to the *Academie Francais* and became archbishop of Cambrai in 1695. There were tremendous titles and wealth associated with that position, and he was on a professional course that seemed destined to ultimately land him a cardinal's cap. But all of this was to change.

In 1688 he met a woman by the name of Madame Guyon, and they became lifelong friends. She possessed certain personal eccentricities and was deeply immersed in a type of medieval mysticism. She exercised tremendous influence on Fénelon. In time he came to believe that the central need of the soul is complete abandonment to God's providential care. This alteration in his thinking gradually affected everything in his life.

The view that Fénelon held is typically referred to as quietism, although as mentioned earlier he was more moderate in many of his views than others who characterized that movement; therefore, he has come to be regarded as a sort of semiquietist. The more radical quietists advocated a pacificity that virtually sought self-annihilation—a tranquility or nirvana bordering on a Brahman or Buddhist type of union of the soul with the Divine. Like many of the Eastern mystics, they argued that the ideal state of the soul involves a return to its origin or divine source.

While Fénelon shared some of the quietists' views, he did not advocate a complete pacificity or tranquility. Instead he believed that there is an ideal state for the Christian where the believer seeks the love of God for its own sake, without any ulterior desires or impediments. He argued that the goal of the Christian life is to enjoy God while seeking nothing for self—self-abandonment. He further argued that this sort of self-abandonment involved being willing to relinquish all personal interests, desires, and possessions. Meditative and contemplative prayer is a tool to help the Christian develop this self-abandonment and enjoy God.

The Catholic Church took a firm stand against all forms of quietism near the end of the seventeenth century. Fénelon's friend Madame Guyon drew criticism from the archbishop of Paris and was imprisoned twice. Fénelon tried to defend her as well as her position, and then he too got in serious trouble as a result. Yet he clearly understood what he was risking in order to defend her. In his defense of her, he wrote back and forth with his former mentor, the Bishop Bossuet. Bossuet would write a book to condemn Guyon, and then Fénelon would respond with a book defending her.

Bossuet eventually became Fénelon's enemy, and when Fénelon published *The Maxims of the Saints* in 1697, Bossuet attacked it as inconsistent with traditional Christian teachings. Two prelates then appealed to Rome, and portions of Fénelon's book were actually condemned by the pope in 1699.

As a result of all this, Fénelon got further into trouble. The book I mentioned earlier, *Telemachus*, was then published without his permission, and it displeased the king. This book, by the way, is what Fénelon has become best known for in secular history, and it states that kings exist for the benefit of their subjects. Louis XIV took that assertion as a direct barb against him, and he ordered Fénelon into exile. He was stripped of his position in the court and exiled to his own diocese. What is remarkable about this circumstance is that there is not a trace of bitterness in Fénelon over his loss. His strength of character comes through very clearly in his correspondences. Despite his condemnation and exile, and right up to his death in 1715, he never ceased his correspondence to those at the court who had become his spiritual children.

He was a man who many agreed was "dead to vanity." As one contemporary wrote, "It was difficult to take one's eyes off of him. He possessed a natural eloquence, grace and finesse and a most insinuating yet noble and appropriate courtesy, a wonderful power of explaining the hardest matter in a lucid and distinct manner. He is a man who never sought to seem cleverer than those with whom he conversed, who brought himself insensibly to their level to make them at ease and then enthralling them so they could never leave him or mistreat him nor help seeking him again." Another person wrote of him, "I have seen him adapt himself within a short space of time to all classes associating with the great and using their style without any loss of Episcopal dignity and then turning to the lowly and young. There was no readiness or affection to turn from one to the other. It seemed as though he naturally embraced all varieties."

François Fénelon was a man who suffered great rejection and grief and yet who was somehow indifferent to the things that impressed other people. He could work well with people of position, prestige, intellect, and power; but he also gave his heart and his life, especially in his last years, to the poor and the destitute. He could adapt himself without being condescending to people. Throughout his life, he was a man of great passion and purpose.

Correspondence

I would like to share with you some of my favorite passages

from Fénelon's letters in *Christian Perfection.* Otherwise we could go on and on, exploring his writings. It is important to understand that devotional literature requires a certain attentive receptiveness from its reader. It is best read with humility and in a context of reflection and slowly enough to absorb its substance. Great literature shares something with great art; both require time and attention in order to see and understand their nuances, and both are intended to be revisited frequently. Just as we would never look at a painting only once and put it away, neither should a good book be read only one time and then set aside on the shelf. It is pleasurable and beneficial to revisit great works. Though long dead, men like Fénelon can still speak to us.

Many of Fénelon's letters deal with the issues of everyday living—temptations, distractions, prayer, worship, and the never-ceasing interior warfare of the soul. They deal with the conflicting claims of self and God, whether we are going to be theocentric or egocentric. This is always a challenge in our lives, is it not?

How do we bear our faults? How do we bear with the faults of others? How do we deal with the unexpected deprivations we encounter? What about the tainting power of self-love or the need of purgation by God and God's severe mercies? All of these are themes of Fénelon's letters. Consequently, he is a man who forces his reader to think deeply. That is why his books aren't popular in most bookstores today. He forces us to wrestle with fundamental issues.

For instance, in a letter concerning the use of time, Fénelon writes, "A person does not only lose time by doing nothing or doing what is wrong. He also loses it by doing something other than what he ought to do even though what he does is good." This is an important insight; it highlights the difference between discerning between the good and the best.

He observes that "we are ingenious at perpetually seeking our own interests," and that is certainly true. He also notes, "What worldly souls do crudely and openly people who want to live for God often do more subtly with the help of some pretext which, serving them as a screen, stops them from seeing the 'everyness' of their behavior." With this statement, he touches on the danger of self-deception and living behind the guise of a Christian veneer.

He also deals with the idea of "receiving from moment to moment whatever it pleases God to give us, referring to Him at once in the doubts which we necessarily run into, turning to Him in the weakness into which goodness slips from exhaustion, calling on Him and lifting oneself to Him when our hearts are swept away by material things, sees itself led imperceptibly off the path and finds itself forgetting and drifting away from God." He emphasizes the importance of integrating the public and private affairs of life in a consistent way and being vigilant in the management of time.

In another letter he asserts, "We should never finish if we want to constantly sound the bottom of our hearts. Wanting to escape from the self in the search for God, we shouldn't be too preoccupied with the self in such frequent examinations." In other words, the hyper-examination of the self can be a subtle form of pride.

He also alludes to a world that is no longer divided between God and creatures: "A world quiet in His hands which neither desires anything nor refuses anything, which wants without reservation everything He wants and which never, under any pretext, wants anything that He does not want." He calls this "a simple will which is entirely filled with that of God wherever His providence leads you."

Here it is important to examine this perspective on the will, however. Many people have erred in believing that the will can be perfectly subdued during the soul's temporal existence, something that is not taught in Scripture. Rather the believer is commanded to yield to the Holy Spirit, a theological distinction that is important. The mystical view would transfer the responsibility of subduing the will to the believer, while the Bible teaches that humans are incapable of such a renouncement of the will. This is the very dilemma Paul expresses in Romans 7. It is also the reason for Paul's triumphant Romans 8:26–27: "In the same way the Spirit also helps our weakness; for we do not know how to pray as we should, but the Spirit Himself intercedes for us with groanings too deep for words; and He who searches the hearts knows what the mind of the Spirit is, because He intercedes for the saints according to the will of God."

While Fénelon's exhortations to pray and to desire God for himself have merit, it is important that we not fall into the error of emphasizing the inward work over the external—a significant difference between Catholic and Protestant theology in general, by the way. The central point of Christianity is not what occurs within the heart of man but what occurred beyond him, in and through God's redemptive intervention. The primary consequence of the fall was an obsessive introspection, and any time we begin to look for change within ourselves, we are on dangerous theological footing.

In some of his correspondence, Fénelon discusses the fact that God often chooses for you and me what we would not choose for ourselves. He explains that suffering and deprivations can be used by God to draw us and even drive us toward him and that it is therefore important to understand that what appears to be bad to us is really something that we must receive from the hand of God. Fénelon asserts that the believer must, moment by moment, enter into God's plans, and he references a "purity of intention" and a desire for a person to be consistent and pursue God with genuine passion and purpose.

At one point he writes, "We are allowing ourselves to be swept away by outward affairs, however good they may be. The point is not finding time to take our own nourishment." Here he makes a valuable point. In a busy world full of responsibilities, we often fail to make time for spiritual nourishment and refreshment. Fénelon invites us to come away for a while, to walk away from the things that would distract us from the inner life. Most of us can easily spend four hours in an evening watching sports or sitcoms without even a second thought, but can you imagine a person saying, "I want to spend four hours tonight, from six to ten, in the presence of God"? People would think that person was acting like a monk! We often regard time spent with God as a great sacrifice, but we don't think anything of frittering our time away on things that distract us and sometimes actually put us in a trancelike state. We certainly aren't enhancing the relationships with those who happen to be in the room at the time. It is evident that the human heart and human nature haven't changed a whole lot over the centuries. Fénelon offers insights that prompt reflection and remain timeless.

In one of his letters, he deals with a concept termed *mortification,* and while that sounds a bit morbid and inflexible, what he means by this term is that we must be torn away from illusion so that we can lay hold of true joy. He is not really talking about a loss, for he always goes back to what we gain by the apparent loss of the self's autonomy. The important thing to note when dealing with this subject is that mortification can easily morph into a works-based asceticism. If by mortification, we mean a death to self through the regenerative power of the Holy Spirit in us (the point of Romans 8:13), then it is biblical. But if that mortification concept becomes the abandonment of desire for its own sake, it is not. God does not demand self-denial in that sense.

Fénelon speaks about the simplicity of a child, "but a sturdy child who fears nothing." He speaks out frankly: "And lets himself be led who is carried in the arms. In a word, one who knows nothing, can do nothing, can anticipate and change nothing but who has a freedom and a strength forbidden to the great. This child baffles the wise and God Himself speaks from the mouth of such children." He uses this example of a child's confidence to illustrate how we should receive all things from the hand of God. We should have a sense of gratitude for the graces that are often bestowed on us in unexpected ways.

He also discusses a concept he calls practicing the presence of God, where he emphasizes setting aside times of recollection during the course of the day. He recommends seeking an inner quietude, free from the distractions and disturbances of daily life.

Again, there is merit in setting aside quiet times during the day to pray and read God's Word, but the focus of such reflection should not be a quest for an inner state but rather a grateful response to the God of grace. In one of Fénelon's writings on this subject, he exhorts, "Let us seek God within us, and we shall find Him without fail, and with Him, joy and peace." Here Fénelon's heart is likely in the right place, but his theology seems a bit blurry. While God works within us through the process of sanctification, we must look beyond ourselves to know him—first through the revealed Word and second through the revelation of himself in the incarnation.

Fénelon then references the psalmist as an example to make his point, saying, "Such was the practice of the sacred Psalmist: 'I have set the Lord always before me' (Ps. Xvi. 8)." Yet the psalmist was not looking within himself for God; rather, the verse states that he was looking before him, or beyond himself. The human tendency is to focus on self; the biblical emphasis is on knowing God through relationship with Christ and the indwelling of the Holy Spirit.

Fénelon wisely encourages his reader to ask, "Who am I and why am I here? Where did I come from and where am I going?" He says, "Let us quiet all the movements of our hearts as soon as we see them agitating. Let us separate ourselves from all pleasure which does not come from God and cut off futile thoughts and dreams." I would call this cultivating fidelity in little things. Most of life is made up of little moments, and faithfulness in the small decisions of life is really what matters. Life holds only so many big mountaintop experiences, but there are millions of character-shaping moments. Fénelon goes on to say, "He is a jealous God who wants no reservations," and "He commands us to love Him and if we don't give Him everything He wants nothing." Once again I would like to comment on our author's view. It is true that we must surrender ourselves and our wills daily, but it is also important to remember that God doesn't love and accept us on the basis of *our* degree of surrender; he loves and accepts us on the basis of *Christ's* total surrender when we place our confidence in him.

In another letter Fénelon discusses how the believer should regard the future. He argues that it would be rash to presume on the future because "the future is an abyss which God is hiding from us and even when it comes to us can we so count on ourselves that we can pretend to do God's work without His grace?" Repeatedly, he discusses this idea with regard to faithfulness in little things, and he talks about "God's wanting a pure intention." This is a recurring theme in his correspondence and one that A. W. Tozer also emphasized. "It is holy intention, not perfection," Tozer wrote, "that pleases the heart of God." None of us attain perfection in this life, but we can characterize our walk by asking ourselves what we seek and what we long for. "You become, at the end," Tozer stated, "the sum total of what you desire. You are shaped by your aspirations and become conformed to that which you most long for." God would wish that we long for him more than for anything in the created order. We often miss out and settle for things that are second best.

One of my favorite lines from Fénelon is this next line found in his letter concerning "little things." He writes, "The most dangerous thing is that the soul, by the neglect of little things, becomes accustomed to unfaithfulness." Here he makes an important observation. Over time and bit by bit, we become accustomed to unfaithfulness in small ways, and there is initially an almost imperceptible effect that eventually magnifies and affects major issues and decisions. This effect is illustrated by the anecdote about a pianist who said, "If I miss practice for one day, I can tell the difference. If I miss practice two days in a row, my critics can tell the difference. If I miss three days in a row, my audience can tell the difference."

You see, a lack of fidelity in a seemingly insignificant area of life can lead to infidelity in larger areas, where it becomes noticeable. Likewise, faithfulness is also typically noticed and rewarded. This is part of the lesson of the parable of the talents. The men who were faithful in the small things their master assigned were then entrusted with matters of greater significance. This is affirmed in Matthew 25:21, which reads, "His master said to him, 'Well done, good and faithful slave. You were faithful with a few things, I will put you in charge of many things.'"

Fénelon writes in another letter,

> People who are far from God think that they are very near to Him when they begin to take a few steps to approach Him. The most polite and most enlightened people have the same stupidity about this as a peasant who thinks he is really at Court because he has seen the King. We lead to horrible vices; we restrain ourselves in a weak, worldly and dissipated life. We judge it, not by the Gospel, which is the only rule, but by the comparison we make between that life and the one which we led

> before or which we see led by so many others. More is needed to canonize ourselves than to go sound asleep so far as everything goes which has to do with our salvation.

He notes here our tendency to confuse Christians and Christianity when we compare ourselves with other people or suppose ourselves superior to others. The gospel of Christ, Fénelon says, establishes the criterion: holiness. Morality—good behavior—is not the goal. When we focus on morality, we deceive ourselves into thinking we are a good deal more spiritual than we really are.

He goes on to talk about "people's fear to advance too far toward the love of God" and says, "What blindness that is. Let's plunge into it. The more we love Him, the more we love also all that he makes us do. It is his love which consoles us in our losses and which softens our crosses for us, which detaches us from all that is dangerous to love and which preserves us from a thousand poisons. He shows us a benevolent compassion through all the ills that we suffer, and which even in death opens up for us an eternal and enduring happiness."

He is not talking on a negative level but about the benefits, really, of trusting what God would have for us. If I had to single out one fundamental issue that impedes most people, it would be that word *trust*. We are afraid of trusting God enough to recklessly abandon ourselves to his providence. We are terrified of a loss of control and the uncertainty of the future.

Frankly, our lack of trust stems from a belief or fear that God is not fully good. If we really believed, as Scripture proclaims, that he is both sovereign and good, we would not second-guess, disobey, or mistrust him. In our arrogance we assume that we are capable of making better decisions than God, in his omniscience and benevolence, would choose for us. As C. S. Lewis put it in *The Problem of Pain,* we tend to ask "God to love us less, not more," when we fail to see his character properly, for we mistrust what he might do.

In several correspondences Fénelon focuses on the issue of man's imitation of Jesus Christ. At one point he notes the ironic contrast between God and man: "The nothing believes itself something and the all-powerful makes Himself nothing." Fénelon then prays, "I make myself nothing with Thee, Lord; I make Thee the entire sacrifice of my pride and vanity which possesses me up to the present. Help my good intention. Keep me from the occasions of my falling."

In discussing this contrast, he looks at the life of Christ: "In comparing our life to Christ, let us remember He is the master and we are the slaves and He is all-powerful and we are all-weakness. He lowers Himself and we raise ourselves." As Mark 10:43–45 notes, we seek to be served, but the Son of Man did not come to be served but to serve and to give his life as a ransom for us. The difference between our sinful and selfish motivations and Christ's perfect love should lead us to a response of gratitude and humility.

Fénelon also addresses the concept of "true liberty." He asserts that "whoever works to let go of himself, to forget himself, to renounce himself, following the precepts of Jesus Christ, cuts at one blow the root of all his vices and finds in the simplest renunciation of himself the seed of all virtues." Yet the renunciation of autonomy is no easy task. Fénelon explains, "God wants children who love His goodness and not slaves who only serve Him for the fear of His power. We must love Him and consequently do all that inspires true love. Happy is the man who gives himself to God. He is delivered from his passions and the judgments of men." This was a major theme in Fénelon's life.

As he submitted his will to God, he was delivered from the tyranny of opinions and the judgments of other people. That is why he could accept with equanimity being elevated to a high position of prestige or relinquishing that to take on humble duties of caring for the poor and destitute within his own diocese, as was the case later in his life.

In Fénelon I see a man willing to say yes to whatever God commands and no to whatever offends God because he understands that his life is really the preparation of the soul's journey toward God himself. He observes the "brevity and uncertainty of life," the "inconstancy of fortune," and the "unfaithfulness of friends." In fact, he certainly understood those things well, given his own trying circumstances. Elsewhere he writes of the "illusion of great positions, the bitterness that is inevitable there, the discontent and the disappointment of all the greatest hopes, the emptiness of all the things we possess, the reality of all the evils we suffer," and he says, "This only skims the surface of our hearts. The depths of man are not changed at all. He tries to see himself a slave of vanity but he doesn't leave his bondage." He claims, "We really need to see, in God, the nothingness of the world, which will vanish in a little while, like smoke, all the grandeurs and their paraphernalia will flee away like a dream."

This assessment isn't merely theoretical; we know it to be true. Our lives are but a vapor. Therefore Fénelon says,

"All height will be brought low, all power will be crushed, every head will be bowed under the heavy weight of the eternal majesty of God. In the day in which He will judge men, He will obliterate with one look all that shines in the present night, as the sun, in rising, puts out the stars. We shall see only God everywhere, so great will He be. We will seek and then only find Him and so He will fill all things. 'Where have they gone?' we shall say, those things which have charmed our hearts. What is left of them, where were they? Not even the marks of the place they have been remain. They have passed like a shadow, which the sun dissolves. It is hardly true to say that they have been, it is so true to say that they have only appeared and that they are no more."

Even so, this is only a reflection. That is why he says, "The time draws near, let us hasten to be ready for it. Let us love the eternal beauty which does not grow old and which stops those from growing old those who love it only." There is the hope: "It stops those from growing old who love it only." That is why Paul could say that the outer man is perishing but that the inner man is being renewed day by day. Fénelon then encourages his reader by exhorting, "Lift your eyes to the heights and see that which will endure. Do not allow yourself to be consumed by the passions that will perish."

He goes on to ask, "What has become of the great actors who filled the scene thirty years ago? How many of them have died in the last seven or eight years? Soon we will follow them. Is this, then, the world to which we are so devoted? We only pass through it. We are a way out. 'Misery, vanity, and folly is only a passing figure', as St. Paul said." With these statements, he argues that abandonment of the self to God is not an escape into an illusion but rather is to reality itself.

One of themes of Fénelon's later life was suffering, and so this topic also finds its way into his correspondence. In a number of letters, he writes about "suffering love" and "interior peace," and he links these character qualities to confidence in God. He goes on to say, "This begetting of self is the most perfect penitence because all conversion only consists of renouncing 'self' to be engrossed in God."

It is not merely a renunciation of the self but an engrossing interest in God—a focus away from the self, with all its illusions and follies in order to enjoy the presence and power and peace of the living God. As Fénelon clearly stated, "The vigilance which Jesus Christ commands is a faithful attention, always to love and do the will of God in the present moment, following the indications that we have of it. It does not consist, however, in upsetting ourselves, tormenting ourselves and being constantly preoccupied with ourselves rather than lifting our eyes to God."The way to get our eyes off ourselves is to focus on Christ. Fénelon's correspondence reminds us that there is a better vision to pursue.

The conflict between an egocentric perspective and a theocentric one serves as a major theme in his writing when he speaks about self-forgetfulness: "When you forget 'self' and are no longer deliberately seeking its interest, we don't regard ourselves for the love of ourselves, but for the vision of God which we seek often results in a new view of ourselves. It is like a man who looks at another, behind whom is a great mirror. In considering the other, he sees himself and discovers himself, without really intending to." Here he is talking about this idea of being so absorbed by the love of

God that we become increasingly dependent on him. "We want to possess Thee but we do not want to lose ourselves so that we can be possessed by Thee. This is not loving Thee." So, he says you have to lose yourself so that you are possessed by him rather than trying to be the one who is in control of that situation.

Finally, he discusses the virtues of simplicity and humility. Concerning humility, he observes that it is very elusive; when we become aware of our humility, we are no longer humble. He goes on to say,

> He who speaks of himself as he would speak of someone else, who does not affect forgetting self, who gives himself up to charity without noticing whether it is humility or pride to act in that way, who is quite content to pass as being not humble at all, finally, he who is full of charity is truly humble. He, who does not seek his own interests but those of God alone, is, for time and eternity, humble. The more we love purely, the more perfect is our humility. Let us, then, not measure humility by the fabricated exterior. Let us not make it dependent upon one action or another but on pure charity. Pure charity divests man of himself and re-clothes him with Jesus Christ. This is of what true humility consists and it makes us live no longer for ourselves but lets Jesus Christ live in us.

Fénelon encourages true humility as "one of those children, of whom Jesus Christ has said, 'the kingdom of heaven belongs to'. A child does not know what he needs. He thinks of nothing but lets himself be led. Let us abandon ourselves, then, with courage. If God makes nothing of us, He will give us justice because we are good for nothing and if He makes great things then the glory will be His. We shall say He has done great things in us because He has regarded our low esteem." Again he emphasizes relinquishing all glory to God, for he alone deserves man's praise and love.

Conclusion

I want to close with this little one-liner from Aeschylus: "Even in our sleep, pain that cannot forget falls drop by drop upon the heart and in our own despair, against our will, comes wisdom through the awful grace of God." That seems to have been the case in Fénelon's experience. He acquired wisdom as he entrusted both success and failure to God, and in his grace, God transformed Fénelon's suffering into wisdom.

Father, we thank you for caring for us and knowing what we your children need, even when it does not correspond to what we want. Yet we know when we see you face to face that what we need and what we want will be one and the same. When we are transformed into the image of Christ, we will want what you want. May we move in that direction of abandonment to your providence as the abandonment of a child into the lap of the Father. May we receive your loving embrace and revel in that so that we will be a people who quiet our souls and move into that interior simplicity with the intention of pursuing that one thing most needful. We pray in Christ's name. Amen.

Also Available

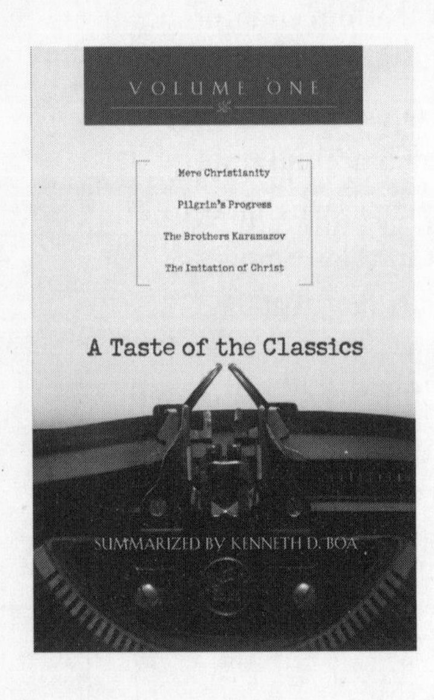

Engage more of Dr. Boa's insights into our rich heritage of Christian literature. See these other volumes:

Volume One
- Mere Christianity
- Pilgrim's Progress
- The Bothers Karamazov
- The Imitation of Christ

Volume Two
- The Screwtape Letters
- Paradise Lost
- Confessions of Augustine
- The Pursuit of God

Volume Three
- Crime and Punishment
- Pensées
- The Great Divorce
- Christian Perfection

Volume Four
- The Divine Comedy
- The Knowledge of the Holy
- Pride and Prejudice
- The Love of God

Retail: $9.99
Volume One ISBN: 978-1-93406-810-6
Volume Two ISBN: 978-1-93406-811-3
Volume Three ISBN: 978-1-93406-812-0
Volume Four ISBN: 978-1-93406-813-7

Available for purchase at book retailers everywhere.